40th Anniversary of Attending the
"1984"
VAN HALEN
Concert

By JIM SERGER

With—CHRIS BERGER, JIMMY MYRES,
JIM MYRES, TODD ZIMMERMAN,
SKIP BERGER, and MIKE MYRES

This book is dedicated to all the fans who went to a rock 'n' roll concert
with friends and can still remember it, and them.

"If I can help a kid discover a liking or even a passion for music in their life, then that's a wonderful thing."

~ Eddie Van Halen

Contents

Drawing by Mike Myres—before I interviewed Mike, I pulled out a crayon and a blank piece of paper and said, "Draw the Van Halen logo please." Without any thought to it, Mike's ability to recall the logo came through in two seconds.

Author Note

This story, and the groups of individuals throughout this book, is a work of non-fiction. Through numerous hours of interviewing, gathering artifacts, and countless hours of accurately collecting data to produce this book, it is without a doubt the hardest and most rewarding book, to date, that I have written. This book is full of events, that had to be recounted visually and mentally, for so many years have surpassed. Every single person in this book I know personally, and I have interacted with on a daily, sometimes weekly, and sometimes sporadically, on a weekend, throughout my teenage years. This non-fiction book is truly one from the heart. I have written and conducted one-on-one interviews with everyone—plus read numerous books, watched countless videos, and printed and read and re-read various websites and the band's websites to make sure the information is correct. We, as humans, seem to remember information as once people expressed to us, which can turn into a foggy memory—this however is as clear and accurate as we could assemble on this topic. So, sit back, and let your imagination, your muses, and your funny-bone enjoy this priceless book—one that will hit home with all who grew up with music. Whether you watched it, heard it, or played it—this book will make you want to "JUMP" for joy.

Might as well.......

JUMP

40th Anniversary of Attending the
"1984"
VAN HALEN
Concert

By JIM SERGER

With—CHRIS BERGER, JIMMY MYRES,
JIM MYRES, TODD ZIMMERMAN,
SKIP BERGER, and MIKE MYRES

Introduction

1984—What does that year signify?
Grade School Friends—Who were they?
Rock Concert—Who was your first?
MTV—What video instantly comes to your mind when you see *MTV*?
JUMP—What does that mean to you when you hear someone say Jump?
Drummer—Which person comes to mind?
Lead-Singer—Which person comes to mind?
Bass Player—Which person comes to mind?
Guitar Player—Which person comes to mind?

Can you replay the line in the movie *The Blues Brothers* when they were trying to get the group reassembled? Well, if you are one for movie lines that pop, then that is what this book is about— "We are getting the band back together." Like the movie, the brothers are driving all around Chicago to put their band back together for a huge concert to raise money for their old orphanage. This book in your hands is what I would consider putting the old band back together—I had to track down old friends, parents, and mentors from my youth, so that we could, "Get the band back together."

I am old enough to remember The Beatles, Neil Diamond, and The Kingston Trio albums (favorites of my parents)—yet, still young enough to remember the first *MTV* video, *Video Killed the Radio Star*. I would say, as any other generation would, that my generation, generation X is the greatest generation of all time. Sure, all generations can match up to the 80s—but the 80s seem to have a life of its own. When I was a teenager—not a single care in the world—parachute pants, headbands, red leather zip jackets, huge puffy 80s hair, mullets, Fiero cars, Paul McCartney was touring on his own, *We Are The World*, Live Aid (Led Zeppelin got back together), Jane Fonda work out albums (that goes out to my mom), Pepsi challenge, New Coke vs Old Coke—it seemed that everything was just perfect. When I was in grade school, I remember fighting with my brother over the cable box, with the wire that ran from the couch all the way to the TV—thank God no one tripped over it and broke a leg. We would have to push the buttons at the top of the box, then match up the buttons on the left to select a channel—as a matter of fact, we even had to turn on the TV with the pull knob on the old wooden looking TV, that resembled a piece of oak furniture.

My life was ideal in 1983. I was in the seventh grade—I was an altar boy at Immaculate Heart of Mary grade school, I was on the baseball team, soccer team, the basketball team, and the football team. I had unbelievable parents and an amazing brother. We ate dinner as a family every single night, right after Mom and Dad had cocktail hour. I was twelve years old—building forts in the woods behind our house was so tremendous, having even helped create a BMX track in the woods. I had the choicest stereo system in the world, playing my LPs and cassettes, plus I even had a dual cassette player, and enormous speakers. All that being said, I was more into sports than into music—my brother was the head banger, I was the athlete in grade school.

The biggest addition to our household, I vividly remember, is the day Dad and Mom bought a VCR. The minute we hooked it up Dad took me and my buddy, Mark Zloba, to the rental store. I got to pick it out, *48 Hours*, with Nick Nolte and Eddie Murphy, was on its way home with me. The minute it was in, and *Roxanne* was being sung, I would say ten minutes was all it lasted, my mom immediately launched out of the couch and ejected it. Her face was bright red and Mark, my brother, my dad, and me all looked at each other in amazement—that was the end of that video.

We never questioned Mom on it, for we knew F^&*, F*@#, Mother F^$&*^ was not going to fly in this Catholic household, more over Mark was Catholic too, and Mom was not going to allow Mark to hear those words. Sure, good Catholic boy is what you are thinking, as my mom had a cigarette in her hand and a beer as well, and I am sure Dad had a cigar in his mouth and was drinking a beer, too—but no way were we going to be exposed to this. Yet, some years later, Dad told me that Mom and he rented *Porky's* and laughed so hard.

My parents, in the 80s, were very hard workers. My mom was a salesperson in a major paint store and my dad was a sales representative for a major plastics company in Cincinnati. They both worked hard and played hard. My dad coached my brother and me in youth baseball. My mom was even the den mother for my Boy Scouts troop, until she yanked me out for putting a penis on my gingerbread man….that's another book.

My parents always allowed me to test the waters, they did not give me free reign, but they did allow me to grow up, a lot, on my own and learn the hard way, by actually going through life. They were not overly protective at all, and my dad never hit me, however my mom did hit me over and over with a flyswatter when she came home from work and found my brother and me having a peanut butter cracker fight—crackers were stuck all over the walls. In my early years of grade school, my parents would always get my brother and me a babysitter when they went out to dance the night away, to disco, on the top floor of the local Holiday Inn. My parents loved music; they loved everything about it. I have a vivid memory of Dad putting on an album, whether it was The Bee Gees, Barbara Streisand, ABBA, The Byrds, Herman's Hermits—when we were done eating dinner, it was Dad's job to clean up. He would do the dishes, took him a while, but they were spotless.

Sports was all I wanted to do! It was the epicenter of my life, like all young wannabes, I was going to be a first-round pick for the Cincinnati Reds. Pete Rose was all I wanted to be. #14 was on just about everything I owned—posters, baseball cards, t-shirt. It was my brother's room that was a museum to music. He lived and breathed music—Pete Townsend, The Who, Moody Blues, Molly Hatchet, The Kinks were always blaring from his room—but, not mine, sports were it for me. I enjoyed music, it was just not my cup of tea. My brother was 100% invested in music. He was taking piano lessons and even received a guitar for Christmas. I got golf balls and a new putter.

It was Christmas morning and all was going very well. The family was huddled around the tree as we began opening the presents—one by one. Dad got a *Raiders of the Lost Ark* VHS, Mom got the Phil Collins new LP, and I got the golf balls. This joyful morning was about to take a turn for the worse—my brother, in anticipation of his gift, for he could tell by the outline and shape of the present, what he was about to open. With big, glossed over eyes and sheer glorious anticipation, he opened his brand-new Fender Stratocaster guitar. It was solid white and remarkable. Now, to set the tone, over the summer Mom had ceiling fans installed throughout all the bedrooms—too hot, with the house facing West. So, with the wrapping paper cleaned up, trash bags out to the garage, and new gifts brought up to our rooms, over and over again—our Christmas ritual continued, and Mom proceeded to make breakfast, while my brother and I were upstairs goofing around. Sitting in his room, with the ceiling fan on, music playing in the background, I asked if I could attempt to play a tune on his new guitar. I had zero experience with music, sure I played the recorder, but all I knew was *Stairway to Heaven*. He reluctantly passed the guitar to me. We were sitting on milk crates, the plastic ones that we spray-painted. We were very trendy. Guitar in hand, I strummed a few times. In my mind, I thought I was already Eddie Van Halen, which led me to attempt a top wire finger slide, while simultaneously using the wah wah bar. Lo and behold, my brother was furious. "Give it back!" "You are done!" "You suck at this!" Well, I got angry and stood up fast, and with the bottom of the neck of the guitar I lifted it up in the air and handed it to him. "Whammmmmmm!!!!!!" The blade of the ceiling fan was lodged halfway through the neck of his new guitar. Then, the biggest, loudest, most terrifying scream was released throughout the house. I believe even baby Jesus heard that on Christmas day. Dead silence for one second. Then tears began streaming—Niagara Falls—pouring and pouring out of his eyes and down his cheeks. I heard monstruous footsteps flying up the stairs and then the door swung open and there was Mom looking right at me. "What is going on?" My brother shouted, "Jimmy, broke my guitar!!!" As if Mom were an ER doctor, she was quick in analyzing the situation, small quarter inch gash in the neck—no strings broken—she proceeded to perform surgery. First, she ran downstairs and got her wood filler and sandpaper, then she cleaned the wound, filled in the laceration, and sanded down the filler. After drying, she headed for the bathroom and came out with her cosmetic bag. Reaching in, pulling out fingernail polish, Mom applied a few layers of polish to match the glare on the neck of the guitar—Dr. Serger was in the house that morning. Her quick wit and skill set, were off the charts and on full display. "Good as new," she said, to my brother, while giving me the one eye stare of death, as if I were Damien. Then breakfast was served, and all four of us sat there with very little conversation. When small chats commenced—little by little, the dark minutes were becoming brighter and brighter—my brother was completely devastated. I had let him down, but Mom had a compassionate way of stating, "Because of the scar on the guitar, will never forget this Christmas." I was broken-hearted to do that to his passion, and I believe that is why I never perused learning to play an instrument—it was God's way of saying, leave that to others, you have your own skill set. Sports and lifting weights. Keep off the stage.

In the beginning of seventh grade, I had a science teacher by the name of Mr. Moellmann. Sitting next to me way in the back, so far back it was by the emergency exit was Mike Myres. Mike had an older brother named Jim. Now, in my household music was passed down by my parents to me. I had no upper influence to understand heavy metal music. In my room, I would play The Beach Boys, Peter, Paul and Mary, John Denver, The Hollies and of course any other titles I borrowed from my parents. Heavy metal was only being seen on *MTV*. I wasn't driving yet, so talk radio was always on, or the oldies station equivalent in the 80s-time frame—but it was Mike, through his drawings that got me interested in heavy metal. Mike could draw anything. He was the only Michelangelo I personally knew. Mike would draw a cliff with flames shooting out the bottom—kind of like a volcano. He taught me how to draw it. Mike was also drawing album covers, so in '83 Mike taught me, as well as the other guys, how to draw the logo of Van Halen. You can probably picture it, a VH, then three horizontal lines to the left of the V and the right of the H. To me it always looked like an eagle's wingspan—so gnarly. I mean it was rad to say the least and Mike could draw this nifty logo. In the beginning of the school year, I was learning all about Van Halen. I had no idea who they were, had never heard of them, but Mike, being a badass about music, welcomed me into the Van Halen era.

That fall, would be my last year playing soccer, Sailor Shooters was my team name. I had been playing soccer since first grade and all the neighborhood kids played on my team. My mom thought it was the best outlet for me. ADHD was not a topic talked about at the time, but in my thirties, Mom said she knew I had it and she thought soccer was a way to get me to settle down and burn off energy. I built solid friendships on this team; one classmate of mine was also on my baseball team and our families were members of the same neighborhood swim club. Chris Berger was this buddy. We had a ton in common—we were the oldest and our younger brothers were the same age, just two years younger. Chris and I ran around on our bikes, played summer baseball together, and our parents were good friends. His dad was another baseball coach of mine, so I kind of grew up with the Berger family in one way or another.

Baseball—every single boy played baseball in the 70s and 80s—no matter how good or bad you were, you could find a team. Becker Electric was my team, and Todd Zimmerman, also my grade school buddy, was on that championship team. His dad, Terry, was also one of my coaches.

Todd and I grew up with a passion for baseball, and his parents and mine were friends. Lucky enough, we lived in the same neighborhood.

Immaculate Heart of Mary was a booming and flourishing school, nearly all of my friends went there, and we had a massive school festival every year. Mike, Chris, Todd, and all our pals would run around and have fun for the entire weekend. While the Zimmermans, Mr. and Mrs. Myres as well as Mr. and Mrs. Berger, and my parents were manning their battle stations—blackjack table, high-lo booth, auction, beer truck—every single member of that school and church were at that summer festival. It was amazing!

We had started school together in the first grade, and now were a tight group of young men in our teenage years—Todd Zimmerman, Mike Myres, Chris Berger, and a slew of others all were a band of brothers. In 1983, minimum wage was $3.35 and the average interest rate for a mortgage was 13.24%.... WOWZERS---the interest rate in 1982 was 16.04% and as of writing this today, the rate is 7.56%. Going out to eat all the time was a huge no-no. Most families were going to block parties, hosting weekend get togethers, hanging out at the swim club, going to festivals, and grilling out in order to save a buck or two. For me, going over to a friend's house was awesome, and I was at Chris', Todd's, and Mike's quite a lot throughout the years. These guys meant the world to me. That is what this book is about, our friendship and the one unforgettable night in 1984.

Influence. Who influenced you in your teenage years? Who did you look up to? Who were you scared of as a twelve-year-old, but today looking back, have a whole new outlook on that individual. Sometimes folks that seemed terrifying to us, were just groomed a little bit differently. Perhaps more abrasive, or more blue collar than what we were used to. It turns out that these are the individuals that I can recall instantly. The loud, tough, brash adults of my youth always seem to be the ones I vividly remember. Mr. Myres and Mr. Berger were these tough individuals and looking back they are the ones who added value to my life. They were, in today's logic, the trend setters. They were not afraid of taking big leaps; they attempted more stuff, or at least to a twelve-year-old they seemed to attempt bigger things than what I was used to—at twelve, baseball was my way of life, that's all I knew. I loved every single minute of it. At fifty-three, leadership, customer service, being a good husband, and being a good dad take center stage. But because of my experiences as a teen—my parents allowing me to cross the busiest streets, while riding my bicycle, encouraging me to be me—I recognize more than ever the importance of mentoring young folks. Allowing them to look through our eyes builds stability and confidence as teenagers mature and venture off on their own. My buddies today are successful, and living happy and adventurous lives, filled with positive emotion and positive memories of their youth.

Van Halen gave me the foundation of moving from innocent kid to precocious teenager. This book tells the story of five fans and two parents, who raised the bar from holding our hands, to allowing us to venture off on our own. It's a side of freedom we all want. It was a rite of passage from a twelve-year-old to a teenager. We were no longer children, we were grown men in one fashion or another—and from the parent's perspective, it allowed us kids to flourish and have fun, while still setting boundaries. We got to be kids, yet be at a grown-up event. This was not the Cincinnati Reds game, not the local swimming hole with friends. This was a real massive excursion, where mystery was just on the other side of the door, and where yeses became even bigger. Our noses smelled a stench that had never been taken in before, where people of all walks of life attended. Most importantly it was an event that none of us will ever forget.

As the reader, I hope you will allow yourself to be taken back to an age where music was moving, life changing, and spoke true to the heart—a time when albums were created year after year—a time when *MTV* was at its highest peak, a time were the top 40 was rock 'n' roll music and everyone recognized the names of the artists, the singers, and could rattle off all the band member's names. The 80s, to me, were when friends were my friends, not just colleagues, or co-workers, or new neighbors, but people I had known for years. It was a time when I got to see my parents with their friends, whom they had known since childhood. My sports teams were flourishing and known bands were still together. I matured in the 1980s, taking on responsibility, having fun, and getting my first job. Although "big hair" was seen as in, I stayed true to my bowl cut, till the end of my eighth-grade year, when I got the ever-stylish buzz-cut.

As you know this book is about friends, and one true moment that was life changing in a positive manner. What I learned moving ahead in life and what I learned to pass down to my daughter, as well as what Chris, Todd, Mike and Jim learned and valued from the Van Halen concert. Any concert is moving, but it's that one concert that you witnessed that is so vivid, it only seems like it was yesterday. I have always been fascinated with Woodstock, having not been born yet, the 1984 Van Halen concert was my Woodstock. I have shared this memorable concert in meetings, in speeches I have given, and in seminars I have attended—long into my nineties I will tell this story. I will recall this day—Van Halen will always be the ultimate rock band. When a Van Halen song comes on the radio, I will always drift back to 1984. I recall that night in an instant. Nothing will ever compare to that day. I have attended great events; Indianapolis 500, The World Series, Notre Dame Games, NBA games, and other concerts— but nothing has been as captivating as seeing Van Halen in 1984.

Spring Break 2022

Florida here we come—let me rephrase that, Cleveland here we come. I am a firm believer in exploring more in life. I always think that rehashing the same vacation, or the same destination over and over does not broaden the mind by any means—with that in mind, I created a new end point in Spring of 2022. I told my daughter, Maggie, who was a junior at the time, that we were headed to a spot that neither one of us had been to before. Moreover, we were going to create a memory with just the two of us, and for extra credit we would generate an add-on stop on the way home or the way up. Now for the record, Maggie was seventeen years old. She had been to Delaware, New York, California, Texas, and a slew of other states and of course Disney—she even had a chance to swim with Winter, the dolphin, at the St. Petersburg Aquarium.

Adventures and memorable experiences are what I have strive to give to my daughter, as well as to myself. Alaska, she has been there! She had the opportunity of seeing the ship from *World's Deadliest Catch* and seeing the captain of the vessel, too. These memories are as vivid as the day she was born. Maggie was so ecstatic to swim with the dolphin, and I can still picture her running around Magic Kingdom, but once is enough. Fresh, new, and challenging is the way to adventure.......the road less traveled.

Maggie and I have been on many road trips, and while traveling I have always played the game, "Name That Artist" with her. A song comes on and immediately we strive to outguess each other on either what the title is, or the group, or singer that is blaring the tune out. The highlight for me is when a Van Halen tune would come on. When she was a toddler, I would play Van Halen, when she was an adolescent and started to ride in the front seat, I began telling her the story of my first rock concert. The minute *Unchained* or *Little Guitars* would come through the radio, I would dive in and share my experience, about all my buddies and when we saw Van Halen, in 1984, in Cincinnati.

As Maggie got a little older, say kindergarten, no matter what song was on the radio, I would say, "Name This Band." Instantly she would blare out, "Van Halen!" Van Halen was her go to band, from house to bank, house to school, house to the zoo or the Children's Museum. Maggie would say, "Van Halen!" It was second nature for her to know longer dig deep, it was a reflex, "Van Halen." She knew other artist's names, she was aware of top forty bands, top forty artists both in pop music and in rock 'n' roll, but Van Halen took center stage.

This trip to Cleveland was a joint, new excursion—having a teenager in the car, getting her up early for the six-hour drive to make it to our destination was going to be a challenge. We planned two stops, one being the Rock & Roll Hall of Fame and the other was going to be to the prison in Mansfield, Ohio; the site where *The Shawshank Redemption* movie was filmed. Maggie loves music, and has always been fascinated by old, run down, abandoned, and potentially haunted sites—from buildings, to railyards, to warehouses, to vacated mansions—she finds it thrilling, plus entertaining. The unknown put a little fear in her, yet she was all in.

0700 we loaded up the car and headed up to Cleveland. We were shooting to be at either site by 1 p.m.—as we closed the doors, she immediately put in both earbuds and hit play on her phone. Not even five minutes on the highway, I turned and said, "Which place do you want to go to first?" Her look was like, Dad, please don't bother me, I need to catch some zzzzzz's—so I said, "We have until I need to hit the rest stop for you to determine where we are headed."—and that was how our trip took off—heading north is all we knew.

As in any road trip, the first few minutes is always small chit chat between father and daughter, nothing major to catch up on, just put the pedal to the metal and let's get there fast. We have people to see and rocks to look under. Maggie, head resting against the door, a smile on her face, as the sun began to beam over her, like a radiant glow—I knew we would bond. We hit Columbus, Ohio right on time according to GPS, just a little over halfway—eighty miles an hour, and we had to pull over for a potty break. Well for me at least, three cups of coffee will do that to a fifty-one-year-old. Can't seem to hold in as long…. we were not in a hurry, but we had to turn two. So, we hit up the normal rest stop, McDonald's. The best bathrooms in the world when traveling. I always think McDonald's has done it right—clean bathrooms, creates a loyal customer—and in me, they have created one when traveling, which is about the only time I hit up Mickey D's.

Sergs and I looked over our itinerary, Rock Hall, or Prison? Which one—Maggie spoke up and said, "Let's see where we are when it's high noon."—Agreed. Once again, we hit the road, this time no earbuds in, so we talked. We talked about incarceration, music, bands, concerts, and we recalled a few of our favorite memories. When Maggie was a young kid, she and I always had our special day of the week together, which was always Thursday for a long, long time—I would get her up at eight, then head to the Zoo, be there for an hour and a half, then head to the Children's Museum for an hour. We would be home by noon—then we would eat lunch together and talk about our day. One moment that I vividly remember is when she and I went to the Naval Academy vs. Ohio State lacrosse game, we made a day out of it—so much fun, all she wanted was popcorn, and the vendor said, "Sorry, all we have is hot dogs." We just laughed and laughed and laughed. As Maggie ventured into kindergarten, we still had our special day, it moved from Thursday to Sunday.

The band KISS was coming to town. Now this was a favorite memory we shared in the car ride to Cleveland. Months in advance, KISS was slated to play, and I went ahead and purchased tickets for just her and I to go together. It was going to be a moment that we would share perpetually. There was a catch to it, the day after the concert was Maggie's first day of first grade. Oh boy, one tired kid. But hey, we had one chance at this, and it was worth it. The concert started at eight—we arrived at seven, and Maggie's eyes were enormous taking in images that she had never seen first-hand. Makeup on boys and girls, white faces, fishnet stockings, leather jackets, humongous hair, "I love You" signs being thrown everywhere, platform shoes, leather pants, and black, black and more black attire than she had ever seen. Here was this little pip squeak out amongst the adults, in an adult setting, and having the time of her life—pointing like crazy, laughing, giggling, and even getting nervous and a little fearful of what might happen—Maggie and I proceeded to our seats, which was a massive rake for seating in an outdoor venue, the stage was set—fire and brimstone was a blaze, and on came the warm-up band—but to Maggie, it was KISS! I can't recall the name of the band, but to this little seven-year-old they were KISS and they lived up to all the hype. 9 p.m., still no KISS on the stage; 9:15 we had to head home—to a first grader, this was moving up the chain fast, and she had the best story to tell on her first day of school.

Sergs and I yakked about that event on the way north, and then we talked about her second major concert. In 2017, Maggie and I went to see Katy Perry. Maggie was thirteen-years-old, the same age I was when I saw Van Halen—she vividly remembered every single thing that took place that evening, where our seats were, were we parked, the giant phone on the stage, and Katy swinging around like crazy, as if in a circus act. It was tremendous entertainment for not only her, but for me and the 15,000 people or so that were at the concert. It was fast paced, action packed, there was fire, it had moving parts, changing outfits, screaming, yelling, and singing. Sergs was right there in unison with all of Katy's songs—I felt like I was in the moment with her, too. Vibrant memories of the Van Halen concert came over me, which I told her in our car ride up to the Rock Hall. She stated, "I know Dad—I know, you have told me the Van Halen story over and over and over." But hey, I was pumped, we were headed to the Rock & Roll Hall of Fame. We continued to volley back and forth musical memories, with smiles on our faces—so much fun.

Maggie and I proceeded to talk about her third concert, one with a festival type atmosphere. She saw Joan Jett and the Blackhearts as well as the band, Heart. This time in an outdoor venue, no seats, just a lawn with a massive rake to it. On the way up, my wife and I asked Maggie what she knew about Joan Jett. "Joan Jett?" She avowed she had no idea who that was. I said, "I Love Rock 'n' roll." "Oh yeah, I know that song," she exclaimed. As Joan Jett took the stage, Maggie recognized song after song, and could now put a face to the music. She was fifteen at the time, a teenager going from I have no clue who these people are, to singing right along with the band and us. It was so exciting to see her joyful and gleaming with sheer happiness. It was so unbelievable.

"Five miles to Mansfield, or eighty miles to Cleveland?" Maggie shouted, "Let's head to Cleveland." We were in the moment—and we put the radio on and searched stations, vigorously trying to beat each other in the name that band game—some she would win, some I would win, but together in that moment we were both victorious. As we came upon the Rock Hall, a sign specified parking was right down by the pier on Lake Erie, so we passed up the entrance, drove down to the pier, and parked.

You had to scan a QR code, then type in your license plate, car type and color, and proceed to payment. All set. We walked right up to the massive sign—

ROCK & ROLL HALL of FAME.

We paid, entered, and sure enough we both were in heaven. There was so much to see and so much property to cover, that I knew we would be in there for hours. It had a Smithsonian atmosphere, to say the least— we were starstruck, as the nostalgic environment consumed us. Down the escalator we went, and our journey began, where music started. We snaked through the history, learning all about Leo Mintz and Alan Freed, and it progressed from there. So much history—history of bands, legends and icons, folks we both had heard of, folks we had no clue who they were. We laughed, pointed, and took pictures like crazy—music was in our blood in that moment. It was so overwhelming, yet so welcoming and insightful from start to finish. Bands from all walks of life, from the small punk bands, country icons that jammed, to grunge, to pop, to one hit wonders, to the most iconic bands.

Floor after floor, we hit it up. Maggie tried her best at learning to drum, while I tried to play bass and learn a new song. Zero luck, but giggling and laughing as we went—reading plate after plate, expanding our minds, learning the ins and outs of bands, where they were from, what songs they wrote, and lo and behold we came up on Van Halen. Maggie and I stood there in awe and read the year they were inducted into the Hall of Fame, 2007. It just seemed to be clicking with Sergs. She now could put all the music that I had shared with her over the years, to the very band that I spoke so highly of—with headphones on, she could listen to Van Halen tunes. She proceeded to the other plaques of the inductees and listened to their music on the headphones provided. I stood there with the other set of headphones, and listened to VH inside the Rock & Roll Hall of Fame. Pure awesomeness.

Three hours into the walk, we were about to head up to the last floor, the tippy top, the pinnacle of the museum. I could tell that this was the smallest of all the wings of the museum; it was so tiny. I went one way, and she went the other, as I investigated the first case, I heard, "Dad! Dad! Get over here—Dad! Dad! Come on!!!"—I knew that voice, I recognized that holler, a cry of excitement. I swiveled my head, turned on a dime, and followed that voice, for it was a little dark up there— "Dad!" As I got closer, I could see a massive glass enclosed shrine, which encased a tribute to Eddie Van Halen—there behind shatterproof glass was a plethora of Eddie's guitars. One after another, after another...... red, black and white stripped, yellow, black and white stripped, plain white, black, and red, and there it was, a white guitar with an oak neck, just like my brother's (only no scar to be seen). Maggie and I just stared in amazement. There it was, the epicenter of all the stories I had told Maggie about my first concert, my first band, and I stood there with my daughter, and I took it all in. With a smirk on my face, I said, "Sergs, let me tell you the Van Halen story." She gave me that look of, not again, and proceeded to say, "Dad, you have told me the story about you and your friends seeing Van Halen many times. Why don't you write a book about that day?" LIGHTBULB!

Her vision was spot on. She knew it would make for a brilliant piece, and with my little buddy, my daughter, in that moment, gave me everything I needed, a "JUMP" start to do it.

Maggie has a keen eye for seeing what is ahead in life. She is a planner; she knows what she wants, and she will do whatever it takes to achieve her quest. Maggie, that day, knew I was searching for the next book idea, the next novel, the next poem—something to keep my mind fresh and in the moment. She gave me that RIFF. Thanks, Maggie, for that inspiration. The muses were speaking to you and your amplifier was immediately plugged in when you saw the Eddie Van Halen display. I looked right at her and said, "Thank you, Sergs." With that moment in mind, we proceeded down the escalator, which ended up where? Well, like any museum it ended right in the gift shop, perfect planning for them, but we didn't get anything that day. It was close to 5 p.m. and we were hungry.

As we headed to the car, we noticed something flapping in the wind under my windshield wipers. Sergs expressed, "I think you got a ticket." Sure enough, this scrap piece of paper was a ticket. What the hell, I thought. We had followed the procedures, even received an email confirmation from the parking company verifying our car was good to park there. Oh well, such is life. We went to grab a bite to eat. Right there on the pier was a Mexican restaurant, so we got our grub on. We sat down, ordered chips and queso, and a few Diet Cokes then started talking about our visit. One story after another, firing back and forth, we were in the moment. We had so much fun that day, and to top it off ate excellent food and were the recipients of a super, momentous parking ticket. I knew then we had created the ultimate lifetime memory. We crushed that day.

Should we stay or should we go now? On our last sip of Diet Coke we talked about whether to stay overnight in Cleveland, or head for the prison to see Andy and Red. We both decided it was prison time. So, we hopped back on I-71, and drove south eighty miles to Mansfield. Maggie fell asleep in an instant, and of course her earbuds were back in place. I imagined Van Halen was blasting.

Maggie was right when she told me to write that book, to lock in the memory forever. Why not share one's stories with the next generation? Why keep it in storage, when it is so much more fun and thrilling to log it into a paperback, which will last forever. I am a firm believer that events are worth documenting; events are worth sharing with others. Maggie challenged me to step out of my comfort zone that day. I knew it would be challenging yet rewarding on the back end. Woodstock has been documented numerous times, books, films, documentaries, poems, songs, magazines, radio broadcasts, and podcasts. People love to feel a part of Woodstock, the tally of fans at Woodstock was 400,000 concert goers, but it is estimated that five million people claim to have been there. That tells us how important Woodstock was to so many people, that so many Baby-Boomers claimed to be a part of it, yet they weren't in attendance. They simply wished that they had been a part of Woodstock. The Van Halen concert is my Woodstock. I am so happy to say I was a part of it. This memory of what Van Halen gave me, is just so moving and powerful—but not just only to me, but to my buddies and the parents that went along for the ride.

The day of the Van Halen concert is at times crystal clear, yet some pieces are foggy. It is hard for me to recall every single moment of that concert, but what I do remember is a solid work of art. March 9, 1984— "Big Brother" was watching me, but when I left that concert, I broke through to a man, a new world was ready for me to handle. I am sure George Orwell was thinking of me and my sidekicks after the fences were torn down, I know wolves left the pack that day, and "Big Brother" (parents) were demolished and new respect, trust was being created. By "Big Brother" allowing me to go (my parents) a new door would become available for others, my dad was my coach, my mentor—people looked up to my dad and mom—I know they may have taken a few hits from their parents allowing me to go, but hey Jimmy had to grow up some time, so why not the present, why not in seventh grade and why not at thirteen-years-old—why push off the inevitable to tomorrow, for tomorrow may never come—"Big Brother" articulated the situation. Screw It, it's time for Jimmy to flourish and meet the new world head on.

Jim and Maggie Serger at the Rock & Roll Hall of Fame—April 2022

Jim Serger doing his rendition of *Eruption*, through the bass instructional
video,
at the Rock & Roll Hall of Fame.

March 9, 1984

Mike Myres, Chris Berger
Todd Zimmerman, Jim Serger
Photos from inside our "1984" Seventh Grade Yearbook

Eddie Van Halen, Alex Van Halen
David Lee Roth, Michael Anthony
Photos from Inside my *1984* Tour Book

I was twelve years old in 1983, and all I wanted to be was a teenager. I looked up to the older guys, guys that were in the neighborhood and were in high school, and neighbors that were in college. I wanted so badly to be older, to get out of this baby stage and become a teenager. In the winter of 1983, I was playing basketball, and for Christmas I asked for high-top Pony shoes, white with the blue logo. I ended up receiving two pairs, one with a red logo and blue pair that I wanted, that would match my IHM basketball uniform. The reason I needed these, was because the Nelson brothers around the corner were wearing these, badass. I was going to be a stud on the court, plus the Nelsons would say "cool shoes." Their older Influence was running through my veins.

The other big item for Christmas in '83 was parachute pants, the bright red ones—man, oh man that was a big-ticket item that year. I did not ask for them, but tons of my classmates received them as a gift. I'll never forget that first day back to school after break, all the hip kids had them on, and they were throwing down cardboard to attempt to breakdance. They were awful. However, it was cool to watch all of them attempt to moonwalk, pop and lock, and try to spin and land on their heads in the middle of the hallway—no skill whatsoever. Michael Jackson was the hot ticket with the girls and a few of the guys, and all the underclass folks at my grade school.

Some of the top forty hits of '83 were *Billie Jean, Beat It, Let's Dance, Every Breath You Take, All Night Long, Karma Chameleon, Down Under*— as you can see, two were Michael's hits. To put it bluntly, MJ was the talk of the school, and was the hit on *MTV* and on the radio for all eight grades. Rock 'n' roll was barely being talked about then, but hey, that was all about to change with a single song that came out of over Christmas break. I remember getting a boom box for Christmas that year. It was very simple, one cassette deck and a speaker on either side. It was not nearly as massive as the one Mike Myres got for Christmas—holy cow, now that was a boom box. Mike had way more experience at rock than I did, so the size of his boom box made sense. He was seen to me and others as the music icon at school. He was in the in when it came to bands, music, and heavy metal. Mike was the go-to rock guy.

45, yes, the Van Halen 45 RPM was released, just in time for the New Year's Eve bash! As a twelve-year-old, this was as exciting as a New Year's Eve could get. *Jump* was the A side of the seven-inch record. The B side, was *House of Pain*.

The music video was released as well—"*Jump*"—where Eddie was playing the guitar and playing the keyboards, how is that even possible? He was a multi-tool, I guess; I am sure the Swiss were very jealous, but hey, he was from California. And out there, anyone can do anything—why not be able to play two instruments on one song.

In early January of 1984, to be exact on January 9, 1984, Van Halen released their sixth album, which was titled *1984*. That day was about to change everything I knew about rock 'n' roll. If you recall, 1984 was supposed to be the year communism was to take over, follow the leader, do as I say. The government was supposed to be able to report to us, on us, and watch us through the TV set, take over the radio waves, and for intellectual purposes, "the man" was supposed to be in charge.

Van Halen put a stop to that in my eyes. They woke up the sleepy folks by putting out one rocking LP, which started with that 45 RPM, *Jump*. They were so clever by releasing *Jump* over Christmas, they got everyone talking about it, and in January '84, with the release of the album— "WHAMMO," it took off like a wildfire—spreading far and wide and it was absolutely explosive throughout my class. The I found out that Van Halen was coming to Cincinnati! They were scheduled for two nights—and decided I was going to go, one way or another, me and whomever else I could get to come with me.

Now, I had listened to guitar players, I had seen them play on *MTV*, and I had heard their music play around my house—you know what I am talking about. The simple melody, the classic guitar strumming, the easy-going tune— that was all I knew, but nothing was like the riff or flat-out jam that I heard on *Jump*. It was moving, it was powerful, and it was flat out awesome. I knew the group was called Van Halen, but I could not name a single person. They were just not mentioned in the house. Mom and Dad were not going up to Kmart and buying their records or putting their cassette in the tape deck—we had Rod Stewart, Elton John, KC and the Sunshine Band and Chicago playing, along with Captain & Tennille and Billy Joel. Dad was not listening to the rock stations in Cincinnati, like *WEBN*. Dad would allow us occasionally to listen to the pop station *Q102*, but for us to really hear what was hot on the music scene, we had to put on my boom box and listen to Casey Kasem's *American Top 40 Countdown*. I put in a blank cassette, waited for the songs I wanted, and hit record.

It was *MTV* that welcomed Van Halen into our living room. We were on trend with oak paneled walls, an oak TV set, and oak bookshelves which housed our Encyclopedia Britannica from A-Z and all our VHS tapes. There, blasting through the TV, was this crazy guy, with long hair, all decked out in some fishnet outfit. He constantly changed his clothes, at least four different outfits, and was zig-zagging and jumping all over the place. He had moves I had never seen before. I found out this guy, the lead singer, was David lee Roth. Then there was this little guy, blasting his guitar with what looked like brown patches all over his jeans with a tiger striped blazer on, completely smiling, while hitting the cords. That cool guy was Eddie Van Halen—the bass player had thin beard on display and was rocking out with a red and white stylish shirt with massive baggy red pants. That dude was Michael Anthony. Lastly, there was the drummer, no shirt on just beating the hell out the drums and banging his head to the beat. He was of course Alex Van Halen. Every time they would sing the word "*Jump*," they would jump, close-ups on their faces, smiling, and just having the best time in the world. To me, they were not a traditional group, like the ones that Dad played in the car, or in the house, or even Mom talked about seeing in person. They had "IT," I couldn't explain it, but I just loved it.

Van Halen was the hottest band in early 1984. I remember my mom coming in while the *Jump* video was on and saying, "Who are these guys? Weird group if you ask me." Then, she would sit in her chair and take in the whole video, laughing, and staring in amazement. She, too, had never seen anything like this before streaming through the television. Before long, she knew all of the lyrics to the song, *Jump*. "Might as well Jump." *MTV* that moved my family into the Van Halen era—and through that experience, Van Halen was welcomed into our house. I always knew Mom had a crush on Paul Newman and Robert Redford, whose pictures were on display in our kitchen, the old wild west photo of Butch Cassidy and the Sundance Kid. I know Mom was eyeing David Lee Roth and Eddie Van Halen. She would sit there, every single time the song was played, and laugh and point and almost get hypnotized, drawn into the VH world, to put it poetically.

My brother always had on *MTV*, and even though I was the older brother he was the one that could rattle off bands like crazy. He knew the musical family tree—where groups were created, the history of the groups, the band members, and of course the guitar icons. Pete Townsend, Eric Clapton, Jimmy Page—but Van Halen, to him at ten, was seen as newcomers to the stage, a flash in the pan, not going to stick around very long. I saw them differently, Van Halen and their *1984* album, made me open my eyes to loving music. *Jump, Panama, Hot For Teacher*…. The album cover alone, was enough to make you question your sanity in a catholic household—a young boy with angel wings, smoking a cigarette, and looking off into the distance—almost as if that was me and my buddies looking back now.

Smoking was still in, being an altar boy was still in, and that blending of a saint with a demon was a coming-of-age moment for my classmates and me—Yin and Yang, good vs evil—as in the hit movies, *The Omen, The Exorcist*, and *Children of the Corn*—good people, can still be a little devilish. Church on Sundays was a part of our life. It was as important then, as it still is today. Religion class was a course requirement, and priests came to our house, to our ball games, and were an important part of our lives. This was true of all my friends. We were altar boys, got dressed up for Sunday mass, and even sang in the school choir. Now, this album cover was the exact opposite of our Catholic experience. The smoking angel album produces all these hit songs, one after another. Van Halen was blaring in the house, the car, the radio and was absolutely the talk of the town.

February 1984, was a month I was so looking forward to, because at the end of the month I would celebrate my thirteenth birthday. I would be a teenager—Van Halen's *Jump* was shooting up the pop charts, and I was growing up as well. I would go from a scallywag to a shellback, as if to cross the equator in Navy terms. And I was an adult in my mind. I needed to prove this to myself and to others; I had to go in one door and out the other. I had to forge a new path, a coming-of-age moment.

The Van Halen concert tickets went up for sale, and some classmates and I were excited about going. We had to attend. It was a must, but how do we go without our parents? My mom knew Mike's dad, Todd's dad knew my dad, Chris' mom knew Todd's mom. They had all know each other for years, having attended school events together. A bond was forged long before I had heard of Van Halen. Trust was already established between the parents. We respected our parents, and they trusted each other and us. This excursion was going to be one for the ages.

Bringing up attending the VH concert to our parent's, was not going to be a difficult task—we all were aware of the inevitable answer, they were going to say no, at least we thought so. We were so wrong. The yeses started to come in, however our attendance was contingent on the correct chaperone. No way, were my parent's going to allow me, or four children, in their eyes to attend a Van Halen concert without proper supervision. Like any suspenseful plot, planning was one thing, execution was another. Todd, Mike, and I had already gotten the approval. We needed a yes from Chris' parents. What was the hold up?

There was one slight hiccup to all of us attending the concert. One buddy was left out—Chris Berger was not allowed to attend. Even though his dad was going to be on duty at the Van Halen shows. With a cop as a dad, a cop that had worked many rock concerts, including activities backstage detail with bands—Chris' dad and mom did not think a twelve-year-old was ready to witness Van Halen in concert. Chris begged his mom, over and over and over. The Pope that night could have been our chaperone, "Please, please, please." No matter how much he pleaded,

Chris was told, "NO!!!!" Young kids are introduced to winning and losing through sports—Win the BIG game, or lose the BIG game, thus creating understanding of winning and defeat. When Chris got wind of the answer no, it must have felt like losing the Super Bowl on a last second field goal. To be so excited to be a part of a team, just to hear Mom and Dad say no—bone crushing to him, I am sure. While Chris was handling that defeat, we were still waiting on "the chaperone." Our problem was solved quickly, when Mike's dad said, "Van Halen!? I'll do it"

Mr. Myres was a professional chaperone—an expert at events, and an expert with kids, for he had eight. He had been there and done that. He understood how to wrangle many kids; he was the sheep herder and knew how to look over the flock. He knew when to take control and knew when to allow them to graze the field. Boooooooommmmmmmm—we were all in. The amazing thing was that all the parents knew Mr. Myres had a big task, so they all chipped in and bought his ticket.

Mike, Todd, and I were all set. Now, we just had to get the tickets the old-fashioned way. If you are not familiar with the old-fashioned way, let me explain…. We had to go to the gift-wrapping station at the mall, kill time in a long line, wait for the windows to open, and finally purchase our tickets. We got them, our Van Halen tickets, and we were ready for the big show. The stage was literally set, we were 100% going to our first concert. I was thirteen and living without a care in the world. Mr. Myres had the van and knew the route. Mr. Berger would be there with a badge on, and my classmates and I were eager for the time of our lives—crazy, wild, moving, memorable, unforgettable, rad—let's go.

BY POPULAR DEMAND
SECOND SHOW ADDED!

VAN HALEN
IN CONCERT

THURSDAY & FRIDAY
MARCH 8 & 9   8PM
$12.50 reserved

DOORS OPEN 7PM RESERVED SEATING ONLY
TICKETS: CINCINNATI GARDENS BOX OFFICE & ALL TICKETRON

THE CINCINNATI GARDENS

Thursday March 8th, VH played their first night at the Cincinnati Gardens. We had tickets for the second night, Friday March 9th. Mr. Berger had already been introduced to Van Halen; he knew what was in store for us. Mr. Myres, having been to Cincinnati Gardens numerous times, already new the ins and outs of the venue. He knew what highway to take, where to park, and how much parking was would cost. My friends and I were in good hands. These two men were our version of Allstate Insurance, and everyone knew it.

On Friday March 9th, as Chris Berger, with his sad monkey face, sat down at the table, before the school bus arrived, everything changed. Something from the "Rock 'n' Roll" Gods appeared. Chris goes on to tell what transpired, "I remember walking down to breakfast before leaving for school that Friday morning. There was a newspaper clipping sitting next to my Twinkies (breakfast of champions, he says laughing so hard.) It was the article describing the Van Halen show from the night before. After reading it, I looked up at my mom and with a smile on her face, she said, 'Your dad is going to let you go to the show tonight with your friends.' But I don't have a ticket! My mom went on, 'Don't worry, your dad will take care of that.'" Chris put into context what had changed, "My dad changed his mind after working the first night of the show, and meeting Eddie, David, Michael, and Alex. He got to see them outside their rock 'n' roll persona, as real people."

Jump was the first song that got Chris addicted to Van Halen, however it was the opening song on that Friday night that got Chris' blood flowing and created a fan for life. Thant song set the scene for what rock 'n' roll means to Chris. That was the song *Unchained*— Chris' memory of that moment is so genuine and real, as if it were yesterday, "I remember Eddie playing some riffs, and then he started the riff for *Unchained*." It was an "Oh My God" moment for this twelve-year-old, having just walked into the biggest venue of his life and the band opened up with this heart pounding, fast, and energetic song—*Unchained.* Chris said, "To this day, if I need a song, if I need a pick me up. That is my go-to song. That is what I choose every single time."

Getting to go to this concert, was a defining moment not only in my life, but Chris' as well—His mom, Jan, and his dad, Skip, knew that they had to allow Chris to grow up. They thought Chris was mature enough to go to this Van Halen concert as a twelve-year-old. "It really shaped who I was, experiencing that for the first time," Chris stated. Chris had never been to a concert before; he had never been in a coliseum before. Chris had never experienced walking into an indoor venue, with all the lights on, and walking down the steep steps to our seats on the floor.

"The first time I had ever seen that before."—Chris' jaw-dropping introduction to folks smoking weed. Think about this, he was the son of a cop, and Nancy Reagan's "Just Say No" campaign was everywhere. Suddenly, Chris and all of us buddies are introduced to a whole new world—we were happening. "I had never seen anyone fire one up," Chris exclaimed jokingly, and with pure comic relief. At fifty-two, Chris has seen a few things, at only twelve and this being his first adventure, he had an eye-opening experience.

"It was a stage of being a kid, to growing up. I had never been out that late," Chris disclosed. "We had sleepovers, stayed out late during the summer, but going to a grown-up event, I mean were going to see Van Halen—we were going to go and see them. It was like when you lose your virginity." Chris revealed, "You can't replace that night, unless you experienced that night, you will not understand."

I firmly believed that getting to go to this concert was going to wake me up, teach me a few lessons, and actually give me more of a backbone in this game of life. This, my first concert, lived up to my expectations, and all the hype. This concert delivered a guarantee. It guaranteed that we would remember this for the rest of your lives, and it has delivered a million-fold.

Going to a concert is one thing, feeling safe and protected is another, but we had Mr. Myres and Mr. Berger. With Mr. Berger there, we knew we were protected if anything were to go sour. Chris recalls, "My dad was perched up in the rafters, protecting us from afar." I know for certain that is how Mrs. Berger and all of the parents envisioned the cop that night. He was right there with a rifle and scope, looking out for possible thugs. Protecting us, at all costs.

"Jack Daniels!!!" Chris shouted with authority, on the question of what do you remember about Michael Anthony. "I remember him playing his Jack Daniels bass and swinging around the stage with the pulley system going across the stage." Chris' memory is picture perfect. He recalled Michael carrying his Jack Daniels bass and swinging around on this wire. Then, we both said simultaneously, "Do you remember him drinking the fifth of Jack Daniels?" Chris answered, "Of course, and the little person who ran on stage to present him with the bottle and he drank the whole thing." To which I replied, "No way!" Well, he did spit a ton out," Chris admits. Chris and I were in unison, laughing and describing that memory to a T. "I thought that bass was the coolest thing in the world", Chris went on, "I love Michael Anthony, his bass riffs are unbelievable, *Running with The Devil*."

Eddie Van Halen—What was your memory of him? "I wonder if Valerie Bertinelli is going to be here, where is she sitting?" Chris revealed, with a huge smile on his face. Hey, he was a boy, and boys are attracted to girls, and Valerie was on a show he watched, so sure that would be a concern of his.

"Was the gong going to be set on fire?" That was Chris' concern with Alex Van Halen, not the drum solo, not the raging drum performance, but was the gong going to be set ablaze. "I wanted to see Alex light that on fire, and he did. The concert was so fast, the night was just a blur," and to put it in Chris' words, "I think we had a contact buzz."

It is fun to reminisce about a spectacular event with your buddies; it's fun to sit down and rehash the events and be drawn back to the year 1984—but to sit here and listen to my friends laugh, well that is why this book is so special me. There are millions upon millions of folks out there, across this great planet, that have experienced concerts with their friends, and probably feel exactly like we do, one great concert has that effect on people. No matter when or where we see each other, no matter how much time has passed, we know that night is sacred.

"That concert, looking back, seemed as if it lasted all of five minutes," Chris shared. Now looking back and piecing it all together, in a puzzle sort of a way, to me it lasted for an eternity. "I found a bootleg tape of our concert—and I all kept saying was, I was there. We were all there," Chris added.

David Lee Roth— "The samurai sword, with the ribbons on it. Him in those spandex pants swinging the sword around, his silhouette in the background." Chris said, then continued, "He was the ultimate show man. You could tell during the concert, that the guys were enjoying themselves."

"I had specific introductions, that I was not to let him out of my sight," those were the last words of Mrs. Berger to Skip Berger the night of concert. Those were the words of a loving mother, to her best friend and what his role was to be that evening at the concert for her son. "She gave me a list of things to make sure he was okay, not to be exposed to anything," Skip declared.

"1984, yeah I read that book." 1984 by George Orwell—like Mr. Myres asserted, he read the book. Sure, he understood what the world was supposed to be like in '84. He grew up understanding communism was to take over. We would see the world through Big Brother's eyes, and their eyes only. The word creativity would be banished off the face of the planet. The word fun, that would be gone too. We would be waking up each and every day to a preplanned daily ritual— eat, sleep, learn. The hammer and sickle never took a stronghold, and thankfully Mr. Myres was our benevolent chaperone for the day.

Mike's older brother, was present and accounted for with his buddies that evening at the Cincinnati Gardens—there was zero chaperoning of Jimmy and his buddies, for he was seventeen years old, and a junior at Archbishop McNicholas High School. He was no longer needed parental supervision; he was a lone wolf, and what all us kids so looked forward to having, independence and freedom.

Think about this for a second, two fish in the pond that night, one was in grade school under the counsel of his dad, and the other was way off somewhere amongst the crowd. One kid was a young adult that night, the other one was still just like the rest of us, sitting under the wings of Mr. Myres—yet Jimmy had free range. He was on his own, no mom and dad to hold his hand, no one to ask him if he was okay. Jimmy was on his own and enjoying every single ounce of Van Halen that night with his buddies. As Jimmy put it, "In 1984, I didn't have a care in the world, I was living my best life. I was working at Snappy Tomato Pizza, delivering pizzas." Even though our circumstances looked different, in this instance we had one thing in common. Collectively, we were all in this together, for just like my friends and me, Jimmy too had never seen Van Halen live in concert. This night was something special, and Jimmy and about eight of his fellow buddies were all there to witness this group for the first time.

Entering Cincinnati Gardens was like nothing we had experienced before, certain things just stuck out. Todd remembers vividly what all of us were feeling. "That place was rocking, everyone was so sweaty, felt like a locker room—people were going crazy." We couldn't drive. We couldn't vote. We couldn't buy beer. We were just barely tall enough to ride the big rides at the amusement park, and yet there we were alongside 10,000 other fans, under the hypnotism of Van Halen.

"There are two things that stand out about that night back in 1984. One is Michael Anthony's solo—it shook the building, and he was playing the Jack Daniels bass. I think he was even drinking Jack while playing the bass. I was vibrating. The second thing is Eddie's guitar solo. You could never forget that. It was twenty minutes long and it led into *Oh, Pretty Woman*. I was thinking, when is this thing going to end, not that I wanted it to, but how can someone go on that long, amazing." Todd, with his thinking cap on, expressed that statement without even looking up to the stars. That image was embedded in his brain for years. He needed no prompting and easily rattled off that testimonial, as if he had been prepping for an on-air interview.

To be thirteen that night, and to still have this powerful moment edged in his brain, is completely astonishing. It was almost hypnotic. It just seemed to flow naturally, like a steady stream of water out of the faucet.

It never changed shape; it never was turned off. The band placed a vision in our heads that night, that in a flash can be revisited. Music is very powerful, but a concert as noted earlier, well that is a whole different subject. That night we were in the moment.

This logo was used all around the stage that night back in '84.

This is an actual backstage pass that Chris Berger has saved all these years,
that Skip Berger gave him.

Opening Act

"Turn Up The Radio"—how many times have you expressed that in the car? Your buddies and you are out and about, cruising around for the next party or the next pad, to check out the night life in the 80s. That one song comes on and you all scream out, "Turn Up The Radio!!!!" That was the indication that your favorite tune was on the radio, and the volume had to be cranked up to the max. Just like the commercial, "Is it live or is it Memorex?" I can still picture the kid, in the chair, being blown back ten feet—that was the feeling of over-the-top jubilation when your go-to tune began to play. Without any words even sung, you heard the drums, the guitar, the keyboard and instantly, without any hesitation, you knew your track was on.

My buddies and I were totally Innocent, going to the concert that night—we really had not experienced much of anything, besides the family outings, vacations, and sporting events—but this night was all about Van Halen—Eddie, David, Michael and Alex. We had memorized the *Jump* video, so we knew all their names, knew where they played on stage, and presumed to know what they were going to wear, and which songs they would sing. Our vision was the minute the concert would start—BOOM—Van Halen would come darting out on stage and blow us away. We were there to see the rock superstars.

There we were, in row ten, thirty feet or so away from the stage, on the floor standing on our chairs. These were not fancy seats; these were the folding metal ones you pull out for the kids to sit at the kiddie-table at Thanksgiving. On the stage was a picture of a robot—a huge, shiny robot—no clue as to how this fit in with Van Halen. Mr. Myres was on my left, Mike was on my right, followed by Todd and Chris. We didn't understand why there was a robot on the stage. We knew Van Halen had hot chicks, fire and brimstone, and massive amplifiers, (Mt. Fuji would seem a hill in comparison)—but a robot?? No idea???

The lights were dimmed down, and being in the tenth row guess what, no one was behind us—there was an open area so fans could get through, cops could arrest folks, and Mr. Berger and Mr. Myres could leap into superhero action if need be. NO ONE WAS BEHIND US! It was the equivalent to having been given an emergency exit row on a plane. At thirteen, it was beyond cool, there we were friends, buddies, classmates about to witness the hottest band in America...
Van Halen!

As it got pitch black in the arena, the lights on the stage lit up, a beam of light from the rafters took center stage, and out came five dudes in unrecognizable garments with unrecognizable faces. They were the opening act, Autograph.... Opening act, what is that? Never thought we would get to see two bands that night, but hey, we were all in. Two concerts, unbelievable, we got to not only see one, but two for the price of one—just unbelievable. Now to be honest, I had no clue who Autograph was, nor did I know any songs of theirs, but live on stage we heard TURN UP THE RADIO for this first time, and our concert experience began.

Opening band, having never been to a concert before, I just assumed it was only Van Halen—but you know when you ASSUME means, it makes an ass of you and me.... Funny little acronym I learned in the Navy, never assume anything. I was completely elated to see this bonus act perform live and in person. It was a customer service gift for the ages, under promise and over deliver. It was the equivalent of getting not just a chocolate soft-serve ice cream, or a vanilla soft-serve ice cream, but the mix of both for the price of one—chocolate and vanilla swirled into one— unbeatable. It's like being told that the ICEE machine with Coke and Cherry can be mixed into a Cherry Coke...awesome after a baseball game.

Autograph's performance was just what we needed. It was the warm-up band; it was the opening act to warm up our vocal cords and get our heads bobbing up and down. Screams, high-fives, and the rush of adrenalin at thirteen-years-old was why I was compelled to write this book. Like any book, there is an introduction, to set the tone for the meat of the story. Autograph was that introduction, sure I had never heard of them, sure I could not rattle off their names, but Autograph was my first in-person concert. And guess what? It was FREE. Gimmicks are all over the place in sales and marketing, free t-shirts to the first 2000 attendees, free bobbleheads to the first 1000 at a baseball game, two- dollar beer night, one-dollar hotdog night, a free coffee after ten purchases, you get the idea. But hey, it was 1984, and we had no clue what was in store. We were given the gift of a free concert before the main event—just awesome.

Today I live in New Richmond, Ohio which is a river town along the Ohio River, about seventeen miles east of Cincinnati, Ohio. Down on Front Street is this cute, quaint restaurant that offers a river view as you peer out the front window. Even a Christmas movie was filmed here, *Christmas Collision*. Every Wednesday they offer the game SINGO, which is the equivalent to Bingo, only they play a song for thirty seconds and with a SINGO card in front of you, with song titles, you, as fast as you can have to be lucky enough to get five songs in a row to win the game. The first time my wife and mother-in-law went there, it was 80s rock songs— sure enough on the left side of the card was *Turn Up The Radio* and on the right side of the card was *Jump*. I knew it was a good precursor for my table and me. The game commenced, and the song *Jump* came on first; Mom and Gina got it right away. Of course, I did too. Then, a few songs later the beat for *Turn Up The Radio* came on and I got it right away. What are the odds that two songs from my first concert, would then show up some thirty-eight years later in the same SINGO game card? Ha, I got them both right!

This chapter goes out to the Autograph band members, who made that first concert experience unbeatable Who knew that Steve Plunkett (lead vocals and guitar), Steve Lynch (lead guitar), Steve Isham (keyboards), Keni Richards (drums), and Randy Rand (bass) would deliver such a world class event. This band from Pasadena, California was crushing it at the Cincinnati Gardens, and we were all were standing on our seats watching them perform their magic. We had no clue who they were, but *Turn Up The Radio*, now that was a song that I could really get into. Everyone around us, the older crowd, knew who they were, and my buddies and I were right there with the older teens rocking out.

It's funny how fate would change for me that night, as well as my buddies, but the band Autograph well, their fate changed in 1984, too. David Lee Roth was good friends with the drummer, Keni Richards. In 1983, Autograph played a demo for Roth, which turned out to be an instant invitation to tour with Van Halen in '84. They would be the opening act. This unsigned band played forty-eight acts with VH, and after a performance at Madison Square Gardens, the group signed a deal with RCA Records. So, my buddies and I saw the group on March 9th, 1984, sixty days into the tour and it was not until March 30th, that Autograph was signed to a record deal. Pretty crazy, and today their hit *Turn Up the Radio* is still played on the radio, and even aired the same year, December 14, 1984 in a *Miami Vice* episode (*Little Prince*). It continued to show up in various outlets, *The Low Life* (1995), *Hot Tub Time Machine* (2010), *American Horror Story* (*Final Girl*) (2011).

To put it in context, from January 20th kicking off the tour in Pembroke Pines, Florida at the Hollywood Sportatorium until April 5th in Detroit, Michigan at Cobo Arena, Autograph played the United States with VH as the opening act. After their record deal, Autograph "turned up" their own radio. That year Autograph released their first album, *Sign In Please.* If you have never seen the video to *Turn Up The Radio,* I highly recommend it. It is very slick, cool, and has the 80s style, all wrapped into one—riding in limos, dancing girls, jamming, singing, running around and even had the metal robot from the concert. The album would go on to hit the gold album mark, meaning 500,000 units were sold. *Turn Up The Radio,* which it turns out the band was not that excited about, and was the last song to be recorded for the album, became a top-30 hit for the band.

Sign in Please was released in 1984, and their second album, *That's The Stuff* was released in 1985. Wow, unsigned, to signed, and two albums released in basically less that twelve months—powerful, this is the stuff that makes dreams come true. Eddie is an icon on the guitar. We can instantly hear one of his riffs or jams in our head, but in 1985, *Guitar Player* magazine gave the "Guitar Solo of the Year" award to Autograph's Steve Lynch, for his fretboard-tapping and two-handed technique. We got to see two amazing guitar players that night. We were so lucky.

So here it is 2024, forty years later, as I reflect, I say thank you to all five guys in Autograph. I didn't know who you were before the concert, but the following Monday at school, everyone knew and had heard of Autograph. To this day, as I am driving around town, or taking road trips, I love having just the normal everyday radio on—no CDs, no satellite. I just love hearing the tunes in a non-categorized manner. It's always a mystery, and I never know what song it will be, and where it will take me. Will it be *You May Be Right* by Billy Joel, which makes me think of swimming with my freinds at the swim club? Or will it be *Mony Mony* by Billy Idol, which makes me think of high school dances? The minute *Turn Up The Radio* is played, I instantly replay that moment in my life where I was introduced to the opening act. Thank you Autograph—it is a day I will remember forever.

Sitting with Chris in his basement, I hit him with the question, "Who was the opening act?" No hesitation whatsoever, "Autograph, Turn Up the Radio." Chris was so quick with that response—zero wondering, zero trying to get the motor turning, in a flash, "Autograph." As vivid and as clear as if Chris had just seen them the night before—Autograph. As Chris and I sat there, we both could picture the band, but then again maybe not. Having seen *MTV* a million times, new bands seem to morph into each other, hard to keep track of which band was which. This was not the case for Chris, as he jumped right in to naming the opening act. It's one thing to be influenced by movies, by radio, by the news, and we recollect what we thought we had seen, but in Chris' basement it was apparent that his memory was just as fluid as it was forty years ago. It was not distorted, it was not hazy, it was crystal clear—and that my friends is the power of a first concert, the power of recollecting in an instance of how prudent the moment was.

"Autograph. Absolutely, I remember the opening act." Todd declared instantly upon me asking him the question—without reservation, without skipping a beat, he rattled Autograph off, as if he was reading a teleprompter. It was instantaneous, and ignited a huge laugh from Todd, as he and I sat in my dining room hashing over the concert. It was amazing to see Todd's eyes get big, and his smile was electric. It was like he was a kid on Christmas morning, he was tapping the table, and hitting his foot on the floor and he disclosed, "Turn Up The Radio."—crazy as it may seem. Who was your first opening act? Who did they open for? It may not seem as radiant today, but if you can blurt it out, good on you and good on them for giving you that ever lasting memory. Todd and I leaned back in our chairs and laughed all about Autograph. It was like a time capsule moment, we jack hammered the concrete, opened the box inside, and pictured us watching the warm-up band. Todd shared, "All I remember from the opening act, was at the end, the drummer threw his sticks into the crowd." Now for the record, everyone loves the drummer, however in my opinion, they get almost no spotlight in any concert. Yes, they get a shout out. Yes, they get a solo, but for Todd, that night, it was all about the drummer. He recollects the drummer tossing his drumsticks into the crowd—that my friends is a moment in time. It was powerful and exciting. That is the gift of any event, we hang onto a handful of moments, and Todd's was the drummer hurling his sticks into the crowd. The warm-up band did not fail Todd. They gave him his money's worth.

Maybe it is because *Turn Up The Radio* is still played on the airwaves, but Mike instantly recalled, "Autograph was the first band out. We were there to see Van Halen, yet we saw Autograph come out on stage first."

Mike, as well as Chris and Todd, on a dime, shared the band's name and the song they performed.

Young kids, innocent, and jumping on the coattails of others, I would say best describes all of us that night. We were totally oblivious to what was instore. We would just follow the lead, go with the flow, and enjoy this new excursion to add to our toolbox of life experiences. As far as the concert went, we all thought we were only seeing Van Halen. Todd explains it very clearly forty years later, "I thought Van Halen was going to play, then we would head home. I had no idea we got to see a concert before our concert." That's the way we all were introduced to the warm-up band, but Autograph was not just any warm-up band, they were opening for Van Halen, and we were there for it.

Emotional Rescue	Radioactive	Fallen Angel	Twilight Zone	Back In Black
Only the Lonely	High on You	Sunglasses at Night	Harden My Heart	Keep On Loving You
Juke Box Hero	Simply Irresistible	Who's Crying Now	Cuts Like A Knife	I Wish I Had A Girl
Sharp Dressed Man	Jump	Runaway	Free Fallin'	Magic
I'm Burning For You	Gypsy	Rosanna	Heat Of The Moment	White Wedding

Above is a SINGO Cincinnati card—*Jump* is on this one. Land five in a row and yell out SINGO!! And you win the big door prize—in my case, a $20

dollar gift card to Front Street Café.
Cincinnati Singo gave permission to use this block.

The Cop

(Skip Berger)

"Go head punk, make my day." —Clint Eastwood in his role as *Dirty Harry*. One of the most famous movie lines of all time. So popular, you can find just about anything on the World Wide Web with that slogan for sale—good Christmas gift for those old enough to remember that fictitious character.

Here is the catch, I knew a real-life Dirty Harry, he goes by the name, Berger, Skip Berger that is; shaken, not stirred. Mr. Berger's real name is Harry Berger, just like in the movie. Mr. Eastwood's name was Harry Callahan, albeit Harry Berger was the real-life version to me in the early 80s. "Feel lucky punk?" Well, I'll tell you this, to a twelve-year-old boy, Mr. Berger was the real deal—no retake for him or shoot from the top. Mr. Berger was a real Cincinnati police officer. Talk about tough as nails, this guy was. I was fortunate enough growing up, that a ton of my dad's friends were police officers, Mr. Williams, Mr. Truss, Mr. Hassebrock, and Mr. Holder who lived across the street from us. I mean they seemed to be all over the neighborhood. The difference was Chris, and I were friends, therefore I would see Mr. Berger almost five times a week. Whether that was at baseball, soccer, the swimming pool, or at IHM. Mr. Berger was going to be around. He was, to me, the definition of the *Streets of San Francisco*.

Growing up in the 80s, mature television shows aired after 9 p.m.—*Hill Street Blues*, and of course *Streets of San Francisco*, starring Karl Malden and Michael Douglas. I was restricted from watching both shows. Mom and Dad said those were adult programs, anything after 9 p.m. was their entertainment time. So of course, I probably was in my room, reading Dad's *Playboys*, that I found in the attic. He shared he got them for the articles. Sure Dad, I'll give you a 10 out of 10 for trying…. Hugh Hefner I am sure thanks you. Great article on President Carter.

Harry "Skip" Berger, was the line leader to me at a young age. Cop shows were the in thing, and *Death Wish* was completely badass. I watched it at someone else's house, where I learned to cross the wires on the back of the cable box to receive free *HBO* for about an hour. I have purposefully left out this family's name—but if the mom is reading this, I am sorry I locked up the box. Skip, to me, was the dad that had all the "word on the street" stories. He could rattle them off like crazy, working up scenarios that I know happened to him, and he had a way of expressing them to my friends and me, so we could understand. He had street smarts.

"Get the hell off the tennis courts, Serger!!!" Mr. Berger shouted at me, one day at the swim club. To lay out the picture, turf shoes for baseball were in. Why I had them, when all I played on was grass, was beyond me. But there I was playing tennis with turf shoes on—scuffing up the court everywhere. If you do that for a few hours, it tends to look as if an Abrams Tank made its way through center court. "Serger get over here!" Shouted Mr. Berger, as his wife, Mrs. Berger, and he were about to enter the cage of courts. I grabbed my racket, waved to my friends, and doggedly ran over to Mr. Berger. In his Dr. Jekyll and Mr. Hyde routine, he changed to the mild-mannered gentleman, and explained why I should not be playing on the courts. He was doing a little reprimanding, and I could tell he was disappointed in me, and fired up. But hey, he was with his wife, in a public place and having gone through his 10,000 hours of expertise, Mr. Berger with kid gloves on said, "Jimmy, you have to wear tennis shoes while on the tennis courts." I am sure I replied, "Yes sir, Mr. Berger," like a dog in the corner getting ridiculed. He was right, and I was wrong.

Chris Berger and I played on numerous teams together. We practiced during the week and had games on the weekend—that was it. It is not like today, where kids have three on Saturday and two on Sunday, it was a one and done. One season, in mid-June, on a Saturday, Mr. Berger was late to the game. Now Mr. Berger was cool too and wore shades to prove it. He coached us along with Mr. Schwartz, Mr. Zimmerman and my dad. This one Saturday Mr. Berger was a little tardy to the game. There were no cellphones, no text messages, and smoke signals had been banned years ago. No string to a can was long enough, but on this day, Mr. Berger was MIA. This was unlike him, for being with Chris was imperative, and he was 100% committed to leading young men. Let's call a spade a spade, he was late.

For the record, I am telling this story the way I remember it. It was hot, I mean hot, must have been 98 degrees that day. Not a cloud in the sky could be seen for miles, and we were about to start the third inning. When out of nowhere came this Datsun 280Z with the T-tops, zipping in from the main street, hurling down the side road of the ball field. Thick hair blowing in the wind, sunglasses on... From the field, all of us could tell right away that it was Mr. Berger. He sprinted across the grass and went over to where all the moms sat—and a small crowd began to gather around him.

After the third out was called, the team darted over there too. There he was, left arm wrapped in a bandage, all calm, cool and collected. Mr. Berger told us he was sorry for being late, but he had been shot with an elephant gun. What!!! –an elephant gun? –the one that shoots four-foot tranquilizer darts through the skin of an elephant. Mr. Berger had been shot. Who shot Skip Berger? Tune in next season to find out. We were worried sick. It was crazy that our coach had been shot in the arm. It looked really swollen, like a nectarine under the bandage—Wow! Chris was lucky; his dad was made of steel. He was fortunate to have withstood the sheer firepower of an elephant gun.

"For the record, I was shot," Mr. Berger shared... I knew it. "But it was a pellet rifle. I could hear it, I felt it hit my arm—it really hurt. I pulled over and I called it in. A little blood, nothing major, but hey I was shot—young kids were arrested. We found out numerous cars were shot at that day." His version is kind of boring, not to take it lightly. He had been shot. He needed a little mustard to his "Berger."

So as a cop, this man who had been shot, was going to be at the Van Halen concert on the night of Friday, March 9th. Who else could you ask for to stand watch over the Gardens, and the thousands of folks at the concert—Berger, Skip Berger that is. I never really saw too much of Mr. Berger during the days of summer. It was just Mrs. Berger and Chris' little brother Scott and man did they have all the cool gadgets—stereos, a LaserDisc, a sports car, a stay-at-home mom, a cop, a VHS player, and a basketball hoop in the driveway. I mean how awesome was that. With Chris living in the same neighborhood, and our parents the same age,

Chris and I grew up similarly. My house was identical to his, only his 2-car garage was on the right, and our's was on the left.

To be a cop, takes guts and grit—to talk and communicate like a cop takes brawn and a bold voice, Mr. Berger was that cop. He could grab your attention in a heartbeat. The uniform commanded respect. Everyone respected cops back then. Mr. Berger had a strut about him of pure confidence.

By twelve years old and being 1983 us kids were all aware of the "Just Say No" campaign created by then first lady, Nancy Reagan. In the seventh grade, again in Mr. Moellmann's classroom, Mr. Berger was the guest visitor. He proceeded in with his slick uniform, shades in his pocket, and a briefcase in hand. Mr. Berger was there to give the seventh-grade class a lesson on drugs. No, he did not have a skillet to fry an egg, but he did have an arsenal of drugs—weed, cocaine, hash, needles, spoons, and tons and tons of drug paraphernalia. Here I was being exposed to the world of narcotics—Cocaine was talked about; weed was talked about, but that day, Mr. Berger was the professor. he was in control and boy did he scare the living crap out my fellow classmates and me. The statistics he rattled off that day put a chill down our spine. It was terrifying, and we learned a lot that day from Dirty Harry. When speaking with Chris about this, his said, "Still to this day I can't believe my dad pulled out a joint in front of the class. It was my first time ever seeing weed. It was cool, but the image of him standing in front of the classroom, with a joint in his hand, is forever burned into my memory." Show and tell in its finest hour.

Mr. Berger was as bad as they come. Late in '84 we had our first 7th grade party, which the Bergers hosted in their finished basement. The lights were so bright, you would think we were in a hospital, but as the music came on, the snacks were devoured, and the mood started to change. Someone dimmed the lights in the basement—I mean really dimmed, then out of know where came Mr. Berger down the stairs, turning on all the lights. "We need to get some lights on in here." I mean come on, no one was even at first base, yet. But hey, Mr. Berger was in charge, and we were only thirteen at the time. What could go wrong.

A Cincinnati cop was to be a watchful eye over all of us boys at the Van Halen concert. Now that is cool. It certainly reassured our parents that everything was going to go as planned. Five years earlier, in 1979, the tragic, The Who concert event took place in Cincinnati. Twenty-six people were injured that night, with eleven people perishing. Three of which, were under the age of eighteen. Thirteen miles separated Riverfront Coliseum, on the Ohio River and our venue the Cincinnati Gardens in Bond Hill. A whole different atmosphere in '84, as opposed to '79. We had assigned seating vs. festival seating. I know that memory was in the forefront of all our parent's minds. It was still fresh, still talked about, and still relevant. With all of that, the parents still said yes, for the hero, the cop, Skip Berger would be there with his watchful eye.

Mr. Berger was aware of the atmosphere we all were walking into; he was going to be looking out for us, and he did. However, he could not prevent us from seeing the sights and smelling the aroma. The eye candy was there, and boy was it prevalent—I mean come on, the *Hot for Teacher* video was amazing, but this was something else. Pungent smell, what the hell is that smell? Like Lynyrd Skynyrd sang in their song, *That Smell*, "can't you smell that smell." I had an idea what it was, and Mr. Berger explained it to us.

Forty years ago, at the age of thirty-five, Skip was a street cop. He was working in District 4, on Reading Road, in Cincinnati. Ten days prior to the concert, the detail went up on the board for the police to work the Van Halen concerts. Skip put his name in the hat, but he had to get picked. "I signed up for it, and I got both nights." Skip in his deep voice reminisced, with a hint of enthusiasm.

Skip's normal beat for an average day was 7:00 a.m. till 3:00 p.m. Concert nights he had to be at the Cincinnati Gardens at 5:30 p.m., as the concert kicked off at 7:00 p.m. He would not have gone home then back over, he would have stayed in his attire, then worked the detail. The concert would have been over around midnight, and he would not have left until the whole detail was dismissed, around 12:30 a.m. Then, he would head home, take a shower, hit the bed, so he would be ready to repeat the same sequence of events the next day. "I needed to make more money, so I always signed up for detail work." Skip went on to share, that he had worked concerts before, road closures, and traffic detail. This was not Skip's first rodeo; he knew what he was getting into when his name was picked to man his battle station. He was there to protect and keep safe the members of Van Halen, their crew, and all of their raving fans.

"I didn't know a lot about Van Halen," Skip recalled with gusto. "I knew about the song *Jump*. I liked that song, that's all I really knew." For Skip it was a job, he had zero expectations going into the first night of the concert, other than he would render his services to the best of his abilities. Then he would go on his way back home to his wife Jan, and his sons, Chris, and Scott.

Thursday night Skip's job was to stand outside the back door and watch the paddy wagon. Yes, this man's job was to throw delinquents in the bus, in case there was an arrest. Skip's job was the roving guard of these four-wheeled wagons. For some reason, his supervisor asked him to go over by the band's dressing room, so another officer replaced Skip at the paddy wagon.

Skip joined the other cops guarding the dressing room. There was no interaction between them. I guess it was an unwritten rule, no small talk, hold your composure, don't get excited, treat this like any other venue— another words, do your job. The first person to talk with Skip was Eddie Van Halen. He introduced himself to Skip. They shook hands and made small chit-chat. Michael Anthony stood up as well and introduced himself to Skip. The drummer, Alex Van Halen, also shook his hand and interacted with him a bit. David lee Roth shook his hand, too. "Eddie went out of his way to say hello to me." Skip shared, with a smirk on his face. This was unusual to Skip, it was rare that band members went out of their way to make cops feel welcome.

Valerie Bertinelli was present that night, Skip went on to tell me—and as Eddie and he continued to converse, Eddie was comfortable enough to ask Skip, "Can you take Valerie to the concession stands, she needs to buy something?" Eddie continued, "Will you keep an eye on her?" "Certainly," Skip returned. He didn't really understand why she had to go, but Skip was happy to oblige. Valerie was on the move, Skip was walking right behind her, within reason. She bought a few things from the concession stand, additionally she ventured over to the souvenir stand, peering over the items. "Oh my God, there is Valerie Bertinelli!!!!!"—some raging fan screamed.

Guarding Valerie, "That was my key, to get her back to the dressing room. I held the position at the perimeter and allowed her to get backstage, keeping the fans at bay. We walked back into the dressing room and there was Eddie thanking me." Skip said, "I didn't do anything, I was just doing my job." Small talk started again, "Eddie asked me if I knew about the band. I replied, not much, I know *JUMP*." Skip was laughing, as he recalled that moment. To him, it was as if it happened just yesterday. Skip told him, "My son is a big fan." "Is your son coming to the concert?" Eddie asked. "No, he is not," Skip returned. "No, I want him to come to the concert," Eddie stated. "What?" Skip said. "Are you here tomorrow night?" Eddie said. "I am," stated Skip. "Bring your son here tomorrow night, and then bring him back here and I'll introduce him to everyone."

"I called home to Jan. She mumbled, and I mumbled, and we agreed collectively that Chris could come." Skip shared. "Chris did not have a ticket!" Skip said. So, Chris had to meet him, his dad, at the back door of the venue, by the paddy wagon. Skip opened the back door and took Chris immediately backstage. And that is when Chris got to meet Eddie Van Halen. "Ah, ah, ah, blah, ah, ah, blah, ahh." "Chris was star stuck in the moment, mumbling his words. Chris was in awe." Skip divulged.

"Jan and I never told our parents that Chris was going to see Van Halen, Mrs. Berger's dad would have gone crazy, it was devil music. Her mom was a little bit more lenient, but for her dad, NO WAY!" Skip shared with me. Skip's mom, would have been jealous, and said, "I am mad because I didn't go." She was rocker.

The Chaperone
(Jim Myres)

Coach Myres, with his daughter Kathy, and granddaughter Norah.

"Fiiiiiirrrrrrrrreeeeeeeee", that is the word I would describe Mr. Myres—from the movie *Castaway*. Tom Hanks creates fire, just like back in 1984 Mr. Myres, the Pharmacist, taught me how to make fire for a school project that Mike and I were working on together. Since I had never made a fire inside a house before, and neither of us were experts in that field. Mr. Myres yelled into Mike and me and said, "I will show you how to make a fire." With that, his skill set took center stage. "Jimmy grab five pieces of paper. Mike grab your boom box, and you both are going to learn to make a blazing fire right here at the kitchen table." Mr. Myres was trustworthy to me. He was the father to eight kids, and the husband to an amazing wife, Barb. So, if Mr. Myres told me to set a fire in the kitchen, I trusted him.

"When I say hit record on the boom box, I want you both, in harmony, to crinkle up the paper in your hands slowly. Then, when I point, speed up and when I lower my hands, slow down the crinkling." He pointed to Mike, Mike hit record, 1,2,3, Mike and I crinkled, wadded up, and shredded the paper in our hands. We went slow and we went fast, it lasted about twenty seconds. He then pointed to Mike and gave the cut motion, with the slit across the throat. "Okay guys, let's play it back." Snap, crackle, pop. There it was, fire. And I mean, you could hear that blaze from a mile away. Mike cranked the volume to the max. "Turn that down.," Mr. Myres shouted. Just like a California wildfire, we had one in the Myres' house, and it was just beautiful. Man, we were going to get an "A" on the project. Unfortunately, I can't remember what we got, but I do remember making fire that day. And I remember Mr. Myres was always there to lend a hand, there to teach and moreover, there to coach us kids—he was a natural, and I thank him.

At the start of this book, it has been nearly thirty-six years since I had seen Mr. Myres. The last time I saw him, was my high school graduation back in 1989. Mike and I were in the same graduating class. I planned on seeing Mr. Myres within a week of contacting him. Jimmy, his eldest son, gave me his number. I was surprised to hear that Mr. and Mrs. Myres still had the same phone number and were still living in the same house from way back when I was in grade school. A huge smile came over my face, and of course in contacting Mr. Myres, I told him how great it was, that he is still moving around the same two-story house. With that he said, "Jimmy, have you priced out houses lately? Holy Cow, for the price we bought this house for back in 1970, and the price we can sell it for, oh my God! We can move, but why would we? We wouldn't be able to stay in the same area—houses have skyrocketed in price. Plus, our four daughters live right around the corner, and Mike does too."

Folks ask what is our purpose in life? What is the reason we keep going? The love of family, and Mr. Myres exemplifies that. Family is not only biological, but it is more universal than that. Family can mean friends, parishioners at church, co-workers, and neighbors. Mr. Myres has an ethos about him to include others in his family. That is why, he was there that night. Mike asked and he jumped right into an instant yes. He cared for all of us boys. He knew all us, and it was a chance for him to shine as an adult, with a youthful side to him.

Ted Lasso is a massive household name across the United States and England, he is the epitome of a world class motivator, a man who can see the best in any moment shine through. He is an optimist; he is a glass is half-full guy and a man who can turn a frown upside down and can lead the kids on the pitch. In my opinion, he is the best coach on television today. Lasso's message is clearly heard by the best players to the benched players, to his staff, to upper management, to the owner of the team, and to the city in which his team resides. Mr. Myres is a throwback Ted Lasso in my eyes, with a little Rodney Dangerfield sprinkled in, too.

"Right now, I've got ringing in my ears."—Mr. Myres answered upon hearing the words Van Halen. That was his first recollection of the concert back in 1984. "I learned a lot from taking the kids to a KISS concert a few years earlier—that was my introduction into what LOUD was. We were sitting way up in the nosebleed section, totally opposite of the stage, and I could just see my young son Dave, screaming at the top of his lungs. His jaw was going up and down—but, it was so loud, I couldn't hear the words coming out of his mouth. That was my first experience with a real auditory assault." Mr. Myres went on, "I learned my lesson."

"You guys all wanted to go see Van Halen, buy me a ticket and I will drive. Being in the pharmacy business, I had access to bee's wax, you need that crap occasionally, and I knew being in row ten, I needed to load up both of my ears with that stuff." The catch is, Mr. Myres went on to explain, "With my ears loaded up, I could actually hear the sound of the concert. I could hear the guitar, I could hear the drums, and I could actually hear David Lee Roth sing. I could not just feel the thump of the band, but I could correlate the sound with the beat." His knowledge paid off; Mr. Myres was experienced.

"I drove—that's why I was at the concert." Mr. Myres expressed. His laughter was so real coming through that comment. Anyone can be a driver, but that is not what being a dad, or a parent is about, and Mr. Myres knew that. It was about his unselfishness to be a part of a memorable experience. it was his way of saying no problem, I'll drive. What this proves, is he was the soccer coach, and we were the team. He was an expert at taking kids to games, practices, and tournaments. He knew there was no difference, it was second hand. It was a reflex. Mr. Myres, had he not expressed an interest, I honestly do not think we would have gone. It was his way of saying I am not going to miss this high-octane event with my son Mike and his friends......plus get to see Van Halen, too.

Having taken the kids to KISS and Van Halen, Mr. Myres once again was tasked with taking the family to another event—this was a new adventure, a new outing. One that he was unfamiliar with, yet still willing and able to accept the challenge. This event was wrestling, to be specific it was *WWF*, which is as real as real can get (to a grade-schooler) and he welcomed the outing with open arms. He wanted to see for himself, he had to experience first-hand, just like past events. Of course, he, too, got to watch a few half-nelsons, atomic drops, and plethora of other monstrous, death-defying moves... But he was the scout, he was the ensign, sacrificing his evening with his wife, to be a part of the kids' journey. To heighten the event, Mr. Myres' bother-in-law looked like "Rowdy" Roddy Piper.

"I was never nervous about taking the kids, or any kids to concerts. What I was nervous about was taking the kids to *WWF*." Mr. Myres went on, "It was that there were so many different walks of life attending a match. It was not just a rock 'n' roller, it was every single genre and background imaginable, in a loaded setting. After the first *WWF* event was over, it was a piece of cake."

Maybe chaperoning a Van Halen concert would be daunting to other parents, but not to this dad. "I remember all of us parents talking about the Van Halen concert. We probably met at a parent teacher night at school." Mr. Myres goes on to share, "We knew each other. If I hadn't known a kid I brought that night, I know I would have received a phone call from their parents." Mr. Myres talks about how some parents may have been scared to let their kid be chaperoned by another parent, at a major event—nope, not in this case. All trusted him.

As I pulled up to Mr. Myres' house to begin the interview, the first thing I noticed was the IHM sticker on the back of his van. IHM... Immaculate Heart of Mary, our grade school. Now for the record, I graduated from 8th grade back in 1985. Mr. Myres still had quite a few children coming up through the ranks, so it had been well over twenty-five years since his last child finished up grade school. What stands out about that sticker, is that it proves to me, and other fellow drivers, that Mr. Myres is a part of something bigger. He is a part of a community, in the sense that he is not an Individual, or a lone-wolf. He has made a pack with other fellow men and women to be a part of the IHM community. A school and church that his family is a part of, then and now. The sticker is a statement that I get along well with others, I can communicate well, I am a leader, and I am also a follower. It's a bold statement to outsiders that this man, this father of eight, and husband to a loving wife is willing to serve others. He is last, not first, and others will be the epicenter of his life. That is a true statement that describes Mr. Myres. He is always willing and able to take on new challenges, new roles, and is able to step out of his comfort zone for the betterment of mankind. Today, Mr. Myres is a Third Order Franciscan.

What age were you when you first took your kids to a concert? Mr. Myres was thirty-nine years old, and this was not his first concert. This was his fourth concert, so dabbling in the field of been there, done that Mr. Myres, at the young age of thirty-nine, had already been to numerous concerts with his kids. Mr. Myres was already an expert in the concert field, yet to me, looking up to him, I would have never known that Mr. Myres had already been to so many concerts with his kids. Here he was getting the call to the field; he could have fumbled the ball, passed the ball, but instead he ran with it. No big deal for him. Why push off to someone who doesn't want to go? "I'll go!" He yelled, with enthusiasm.

When I asked him what he remembers about the Van Halen concert in '84, this good Catholic man said, "The size of the speakers. Jesus criminy, they were like guns pointing at you." Mr. Myres recollected. My dad always said, there are two places on the planet where priests are allowed to cuss. One is on the golf course and the other is at Notre Dame games. In this case, Mr. Myres being a man of Spirit, was allowed to be overwhelmed by the magnitude of the speakers. They were beyond massive, and if you have never stared down a German Big Bertha, well this would be the equivalent. Mr. Myres, was not one to be easily impressed. He had seen the world, been to numerous concerts and sporting events, but this night, Van Halen blew him away. He was impressed.

What is one more thing? What is one more coaching gig? What is one more plate of food at the table? This is the mindset of folks who take on so much under one umbrella. It's the stretching of a dollar bill, the carpooling of kids to practice and one more late night of homework. This is how Mr. Mrs. Myres' brains worked. It's just one more thing, no big deal to us, we are used to this. We can handle this, no obstacle is too big, and the little speedbumps in life are easy to overcome and enjoy, so we might as well say yes. Overextended? Not the parents that have one kid or two, but the ones with a house full of kids are the ones that always seem to say yes, why not? The overextended families always jump in, always say why not? That was Mr. Myres, lending a hand again and again and again, as a chaperone, a coach, a father, and a husband.

We are all aware that weekends seem to be the busiest at any hospital. And to get a weekend night off, is not simply luck. It must be preplanned. So, it was not just a coincidence that Mr. Myres had Friday March 9th off. He had to play switcheroo—Choosing to be a pharmacist at a hospital proved to be the right vocation for him. It enabled him to be a part of his kids' lives, and a part of his family's activities. It took a ton of sacrifice and it never seemed to bother Mr. Myres at all. "Pharmacist, I was a pharmacist from 1972 till 2013—My dad was a pharmacist. Pharmacy has allowed me to do the things I wanted." Mr. Myres disclosed to me.

Looking up to others is what we do at a very young age. Our parents are our guideposts; they ultimately allow us to ebb and flow, to choose a path, and encourage us to follow our dreams. That is exactly what Mr. Myres saw in his dad. He gave him the seed, planted it, watered it, and nurtured it to life—I sat in Mr. Myres' dining room while conducting this interview and I asked him, "What are you?" He took a moment, then said, "I was a pharmacist, but I was a soccer coach. Working in a hospital, unlike retail, it allowed me to switch schedules with people, so I could make it to every soccer game. As a coach, it would take me the rest of the year to pay people back. You wanted that Saturday off, that was really important to you, so you will have to cover two days for me. No problem." Mr. Myres explained to me, "Two for one." Yes, that was the penalty Mr. Myres sometimes had to pay for switching his schedule with others. Others would take his one day, and he in return would have to pay them back two days. Ridiculous, but that is how it was. Mr. Myres knew that, jumped all over it, and eagerly made this lopsided exchange to benefit his family. The sacrifice he rendered, benefited us four kids too.

Let's all just say it, Mr. Myres was a drug dealer. He was an expert in the pharmaceutical field, forty years in that industry and with the same hospital. Not once jumping ship, getting another job, or searching for the perfect job, but understanding that every job has its perks, and he found them. Those perks are irreplaceable as a young father with a wife raising eight kids. He understood the good, far outweighed the bad. "I coached all the kids growing up, and I coached TOP (The Outreach Program) soccer for my youngest Joe, for fifteen years. I would rather be known as a soccer coach, than a pharmacist."

That statement touched me. Mr. Myres knew what his mission in his life was, to be around his kids, be around other kids, and to have a positive impact in their lives in one fashion or another. People search a lifetime to find meaning in their lives. Yet, Mr. Myres knew his calling long ago, and he fulfilled his mission.

In speaking with his son, Mike, about the role of a chaperone, Mike recalled the KISS concert. "My dad took us kids, (Jimmy, Mike, and his younger brother Dave) and some of Jimmy's friends down to the Cincinnati Gardens. As far as a chaperone goes, I can recall my dad had us all huddled up and walking in a circle to and from the car to the venue. He was watching us all. I can still remember that." Here it is 2023, and Mike can still see his dad standing watch over his family. That was Mr. Myers. On guard, always, standing his post.

As I interviewed Mr. Myres, I playfully asked him, "I have five kids that would love to see Van Halen, can you take them please? If that was true, could you commit to chaperoning them as quickly as you did back in '84?" Without hesitation, Mr. Myres said, "Absolutely. Hell yes. Let's go to a soccer match." That my friends is a man who trusts his instincts, his abilities, and one who has confidence—a true leader.

The Sales Manager

(Chris Berger)

Summer '83 baseball.

How cool is it to have a friend, whose family dynamics are nearly identical to mine. Chris was my age. His dad was my dad's age. His mom was my mom's age, and his brother Scotty was my brother's age. We lived in the same type of house, went to the same school, lived in the same neighborhood, and were on the same team. We were members at the same swim club and went to the same church. Kind of spooky if you ask me, but as a kid, tons of fun.

The one thing that always makes me laugh when I hear the name "Chris Berger" was back in the early 80s *Friday the 13th* came out on *HBO* and Chris had *HBO*. So, there we were watching a rated "R" movie in his family room, his mom was nowhere in sight. When we were about thirty minutes into the movie, Mrs. Berger appeared. She immediately saw the blood and guts and Kevin Bacon was more than 400 degrees of separation—Click. It was turned off. I think we watched the *Smurfs* or *He-Man* or even *GI-Joe* cartoons—no more Camp Crystal Lake. After reading this part, Chris had to add the Catholic values of the Berger family, which the Serger, Mryes and Zimmerman families could attest to, as well. "My mom and dad taped *Friday the 13th* off *HBO*—I kept begging my mom for weeks to let us all watch it. My mom fired back, 'No, never, you kids are too young to see a movie like that.' Lo and behold, one day she let us all watch it. I thought, what changed her mind?" Chris revealed the reason, "Yeah, we all wanted to see the blood and guts, but as teenage boys, the sex scenes were on top of our minds. We popped the VHS tape in, movie starts. I can't remember how far into the movie it happened, but the story was building up to the first "sex" scene. As soon as the girl is about to take her top off, suddenly Bob Barker and *The Price is Right* comes on. Did someone hit something to change the channel??? What is going on? After a couple of minutes, the movie comes back on, and we are into the next scene. We rewound the tape and there was Bob Barker again. What the heck is going on?" Chris' mom, not wanting him to see the "sex" scenes, taped over each one of them. She kept all the slashing, blood, and killing scenes, but Chris sure as hell was not going to see any boobies. As Chris says, "I guess that was the lesser of two evils...LOL."

In 1985, we graduated from eighth grade, and Chris continued his education at Anderson High School. This is where we went our separate ways. We would see each other here and there throughout high school, and we always connected on the football frilled, for our schools were rivals. My senior year, my school was 0-9 in football, we were just flat out awful, but Chris' team was 5-4. All they had to do was beat us, and they were off to the playoffs. (Maybe) My tiny school of 800 was going head-to-head with a school of 2,500. The night of the game, it was pouring down rain, it was a monsoon. In practice, we had rehearsed a play over and over, which was a screen to the opposing team's full back, who happened to be Chris Berger. It was third down and two, raining sideways, when I looked at my teammate, Dave Myres, Mr. Myres' other son, I said to him, "Once they hike the ball, you take two steps back and be ready to defend against the screen." Sure enough, as we rehearsed, Anderson did the middle screen and Dave smothered Chris with a one-yard gain—the point of this story is to shed light, that the Bergers, Myres and Sergers were still bound together. I know that Dave was thrilled with the big play. We beat them 8-6.

Back in fall of 2022, I reached out to Chris about putting this book together. I explained the idea and the concept and without explaining any further, Chris was 100% in. We just started talking like two roosters on the front porch about our night back in 1984. We never skipped a beat, laughing, reciting Van Halen songs, recalling videos, and pulling out memorabilia. We talked for over an hour and half. Here we both were fifty-one years old, having the time of our lives, chatting on the phone about a night that still has so much meaning to us. Yet, I had not seen Chris in nearly thirty years, but in the moment, it seemed like we were living right next door to each other.

We scheduled a night for me to go over to his house and interview him. The minute he opened the door, a huge smile came over his face and mine simultaneously. We gave each other a huge hug. We began talking immediately, as he motioned me to the basement. "Let's head on down to the man cave," he conveyed. He led the way, and the minute I touched down on the basement carpet there it was, the shrine of all shrines, mounted up on his wall. Van Halen memorabilia like I have never seen. I knew Chris was still a fan, he told me so in our conversation, but upon entering I was instantly taken back to the *MTV* era, the Van Halen era and the Rock & Roll Hall of Fame. I was completely overwhelmed, and taken aback at the autographs, posters, guitar pics, and album covers. And of course, Chris was floating on cloud nine.

It was like we were twelve-year-old boys again, and the year was 1984. We could not shut up—our lips were rattling information off so quickly, and yet we both were keeping up with each other, talking about the significance of his collage of Van Halen memorabilia. It's one thing to have a few posters up, but this was a barrage of information overload—it was like Chris had been a roadie for Van Halen. He showcased everything imaginable and then some more...but the one thing that clearly jumped out was the collection of material he was able to save throughout the years. He had rock magazines, t-shirts, pics, drumsticks, pictures, and he even had a photo album of newspaper articles from in the *Cincinnati Enquirer* covering our Van Halen concert. I was in the same boat as Chris when it came to memorabilia, only mine was baseball. I had it all, bobbleheads, pennant flags, baseball cards and so on and so on, but Chris' display in his basement was earth shattering. It is a true museum to his favorite rock band of all time.

That first concert clearly paved the way for a future love of Van Halen and rock in general. It is a true testament to the boys of Van Halen— Eddie, David, Michael, and Alex. That night in 1984, set the next forty years up for Chris with a passion of Rock & Roll. While sitting there at Chris' basement bar, he told me the story about how moving it was to see Wolfgang Van Halen in concert, and that he so wanted to reach out to him and tell him, that his love for music, Van Halen, and for Eddie (his dad) was the reason he became a rock & roll junkie. Chris knows all the songs, knows all the albums, knows all the history of the band, and that he wanted Wolfgang to understand that Van Halen gave him so much back in 1984. It literally changed his life.

To be a cop, you must enjoy talking to people, as Skip does. To enjoy being in a newsroom, you also must enjoy talking with people, as his mom Jan did. Today Chris is a sales manager for a distributor of architectural aluminum products. He has been doing this for three years and has been in the sales industry since the age of fourteen, when he sold hot dogs and hamburgers at Indian Hill Swim & Tennis Club. "I have always loved interacting with people," Chris confessed. "I travel like crazy; I have seen almost every area of the United States. I have been to forty-one states, give me a couple of years and I will have seen them all. I need to get to Alaska and to Hawaii—we do have customers there, so I will make it." Chris is a road warrior.

Merriam-Webster defines road warrior as:

A person who travels frequently especially on business

Back in 1984, Van Halen traveled extensively. Today at age fifty-three, Chris now travels endlessly, hitting all corners of the states, week after week and month after month. In reality Chris is on tour, just before interviewing him, he took his wife Molly out to San Diego to be together on one of his west coast trips. Pretty cool, just like a band, Chris is seeing many cities and many states. Sometimes traveling solo or as a duet. Either way, Chris is now living the life of a road warrior in one fashion or another.

The Buyer (Mike Myres)

Mark Zloba, Jim Serger and Mike Myres—8th grade graduation.

When I think of Mike Myres, beyond the Van Halen concert, I remember him and me being very close. We were the definition of the word buddies. We played on IHM's baseball team together and played on the IHM's basketball team together. One of things that always stood out about Mike, was how large, and how close his family was, and I envied that. He had an older brother, Jim, younger brother, Dave, who was one year younger than me, then it trickled down from there. I wanted many brothers and sisters. I mean, how fun must it be to always have something to do with your siblings. I am sure a few squabbles took place, but the sheer love of that family was genuine. Mom, Barb, always had a kid in her arms as I recollect, and she was always on the go, go go—she was the real housewife of Cincinnati…

Back in grade school, in the fall of '83, I vividly remember that I entered my first science fair. Me, out of all people, trying to display the science of some item, well that was just was not who I was. School took the back seat. It was sports first, then second, then third, school was not even in the top 5. That year, I decided I would step out of my comfort zone, and Mike was right there with me. The two of us decided to take this challenge head on. From my perspective, science fairs were all about the solar system, eco-systems, a tornado, a tsunami, or a world-famous volcano. I did none of that. I took on *The Science of Hitting*, by Ted Williams. Mike took on an old barn. This barn was faded red, the wood was rotting, the roof was collapsing, and it sat in our community at the corner of Nagel Road and State Road.

All I did was copy the hitting chart of a strike zone on to a huge white piece of paper, and color in the circles for where the pitch would lower or increase a player's batting average. Mike explored the art of an old building. Now I don't know how Mike scored, but I was given a D+. No real science to my fair project. I just transferred my strike zone over. The sheer laughter from Mike to me, was hilarious—we were laughing so hard when we walked out of the presentation. For the record, Mike's barn is knocked down and a little park sits there now. So, when I drive by it, which I do often, I think of Mike, the barn, and the fun we had at our one and only science fair.

Mike and I had always been close. In the Spring of 1992, I decided, after earning my college degree, that I would join the Navy—April 16, 1992, I shipped out, but not before Mike Myres gave me a call and shared, that he and all my high school buddies were throwing me a going away party. Mike pulled up in his Jeep, with the top off, and oversized wheels—off we went to the shindig. I can't tell you much about what happened, other than they were getting me trained for drinking like a sailor. I was well prepared because of that night. It was Mike who planned it all, picked me up, shuttled me over, and threw one hell of a party in my honor. Thank you, Mike.

In grade school, as part of our gym class, Mike and I were part of an elite group. It was called, the non-listening group. now for the record, our little grade school did not have a gym, so we were bussed over to a public grade school where we were under the supervision of one tough SOB. He was a former NFL player for the Philadelphia Eagles, and he was a drill sergeant. Boys being boys, we were not going to allow him to boss us around. Sure enough, he created the non-listening group. He would start each class with, "Here is a football. I will punt it. Wherever it lands, is where the non-listening group will stay." So, we were rewarded for acting like idiots. We were the big athletes, too cool for the others. So, for an hour, we got to goof-off. We eventually caved, and we were allowed back in with our peers. But we were rebels, to say the least.

In seventh grade I got really close to one of my uncles, who was quite the outdoorsman, as he had all the gear possible. He even owned a Jeep. He was kind enough to give me one of his buck knives, which at this point in my life was the first deadliest weapon I had owned since my nun chuck's, which my parents were well aware off. However, a knife—well my family was not exactly the off-the-grid type. Dad never served in the military and mom could bake great cookies. To describe their spirit. But a knife, I had to keep it hidden. At school I described my dilemma to Mike, which he understood. The next day, he handed me a hollowed-out Language Arts book, which was completely *Mission: Impossible*. And there in full display, blending in with all my other books on my desk was this hidden gem. No one knew it, but I was all set defend our house, thanks to Mike.

Today Mike is as dedicated to his family, as his parents were, the apple did not fall far from the tree. Mike is the proud father of five kids. Four boys and one girl, which is like managing a basketball team. Mike is a buyer for a major university, where he helps to manage the university's spending. From finding the best price on new turf for the fields, to bidding out health insurance, Mike has a lot of responsibility. Mike put it into perspective, "I have a whole bunch to do, but it is divided between four of us."

The
Operations Manager

(Todd Zimmerman)

Summer of '83 baseball

Todd and I lived on opposite ends of the neighborhood in Summit Estates. He lived on the far westside with woods in his backyard, and I lived on the far eastside of Summit, with some woods in my backyard. We each offered our buddies something unique when they would come over. We had zero folks living behind us, and if we had too much of each other, or felt cooped up, we would take off on our bikes and hit the woods. We would venture off and do our BMXing, and long before mountain biking was even heard of in Cincinnati. Todd and I were on the same baseball teams, with Chris Berger and Mr. Zimmermann was a coach of mine. We belonged to the same swim club, too. Needless to say, Todd's family and my family were close.

Todd had the one thing I always thought was beyond cool growing up as a kid. Todd's room was in the basement, and the basement was finished! You walked downstairs and straight ahead was Todd's room. I mean come on, how cool was that. Upstairs, parents could do their business, and Todd could escape to the dungeon, escape reality, and really go off and be on his own in a whole separate wing of the complex. Todd's room was just like all of my other friends' rooms. He had baseball stuff up, beer cans on display, awards from swimming, Reds pennant flags, Bengals Super Bowl posters, and of course he had a very cool stereo as well. Todd's walls were the old faux wood paneling, just like my parents had up in our family room. I mean Todd was in on interior decorating, only with nails, scotch tape, and cut outs of all his accomplishments in sports.

Todd and I were riding buddies and were so cool that we even got to ride our bikes to school on the last day. That is choice! Todd's other coolest amenity was that there was a baseball field right across the street from his house. All our buddies would ride bikes to Todd's, then we would walk over to the field and play a pick-up game of baseball. We would play football over there too and when it snowed, man that field was the best for creating snowmen.

Todd was the oldest and had three younger sisters. Mr. Zimmerman and Todd were truly outnumbered, 4-2, yet Todd was the big brother, having to lead the squad in one fashion or another. I was envious of Todd, because he had a huge family, four kids. I bet those Christmas mornings lasted forever, opening up all those gifts. Mr. and Mrs. Zimmerman, I just loved them. Mr. Zimmerman was a Veteran of the U.S. Coast Guard, and I respected that. His was was a strong leader, not only in Todd's life, but mine too.

There is something unique about being involved in the military, being a part of a band of brothers, being a part of a mission together, and overcoming the word fear. Mr. Zimmerman displayed that, lived that, and exemplified that through Todd's eyes as well as mine. Mr. Zimmerman had a way about him, he was firm but fair, had discipline, and guys. Yet, he had a relaxed demeanor to him—sure I heard him yell at Todd and us, but it was never violent, it was simply because he expected more from us kids. He was the drill sergeant, with equal parts of compassion and understanding.

Camping, I hate camping—boy do I ever hate it. It seems as if every single time I camp it rains, and the minute it does, I am taken back to East Fork State Park with the Zimmerman family. It was the summer of '82, we just got done playing baseball, and we were off to my first camping adventure. Yes, this would be the first time I would spend the night in a tent, in the woods. We settled into our base camp, and then we felt a few rain drops, nothing major—no doppler radar back then. When out of nowhere a monsoon hit. It was cold, damp, and muggy, and we were suffering. All that crap you never want to happen when camping, well it was present, and it was flat out miserable. Every time I hear the word camping, I thank the Zimmerman's for my ability to book a hotel.

Back in January of 2023, I invited Todd over to my house to start the interview process. He pulled up to the house and the first thing I noticed was Todd's U.S. Navy license plate and his University of Cincinnati bearcat paw in his back window. I walked out, and the minute he stepped up to the sidewalk, we hugged—a smile once again between two buddies was as clear as day. A pat on the back, a handshake would have sufficed, but no, we went right into a hug. Powerful, in that we are still buddies, still excellent friends, and still have happy go lucky smiles.

To get to go to a concert is pure luck of the draw back in the 80s—all parents were working hard, raising kids, feeding numerous mouths and yet, at the same time trying to allow the older kids to grow and venture out into this world. So, to personally attend a concert at the age of thirteen that was a big deal, but in Todd's case to see the very band that he idolized, well that is a plot of a movie. "1984, Van Halen was my first concert," Todd expressed with a pure glow to him. He was so proud, so enthusiastic to share that with me. Now for the record, there were various places we could see concerts around town. There was Riverfront Coliseum, which was located in downtown Cincinnati, by the Ohio River, and then there was also Timberwolf, located about twenty-five miles north of Cincinnati at Kings Island amusement park. Both places had major bands play, but this night was different for Todd, because he was with his buddies, and we were in row ten at the famous Cincinnati Gardens.

To be thirty feet away from the stage and to see Eddie and David, well that is a special gift by anyone's standards. Back in '84, our tenth-row seats cost us $12.50. Today those same seats would cost more than a thousand dollars, possibly even more depending on who you are going to see. The question that Todd always wondered was, "How in the hell, did I get my parents to buy floor seats?" Todd and I laughed, no computers or internet back then, we had to go to the local mall, and wait in line and purchase the tickets. To this day, none of us know how we got tenth-row seats. "Floor seats," as Todd put it, but that was us doing the impossible that night. It was like a magic carpet ride, not knowing where it was going to lead us—that's why it was so special.

Imagine yourself at thirteen, now imagine yourself at thirteen at a major gig, in row ten watching the hottest band. Todd had been to numerous events leading up to this moment. "In 1981, the All-Star Game was in Cleveland, and my grandpa took me there—that was the biggest thing I had been to before Van Halen. Then again in 1981, I was at The Freezer Bowl, Bengals vs Chargers, at Riverfront Stadium," Todd shared. The temperature that day, by the Ohio River, was minus 59°F below zero. Another major event that was going on in the early 80s was *WWF*. Wrestle Mania was the craze, and Todd told me, "*WWF* was coming to town, and my dad took me—Hulk Hogan was there." Sports, as you can tell, was a way of life for Todd, that's all that consumed him—the excitement of the arena was in Todd's blood. But something new, something raw and fresh was about to release the Kraken. "I had experienced going to big events, but nothing quite on the level of a Van Halen concert." Todd nodded to me, as he told me his calendar of events, it was a new fresh door that was opened into Todd's life for the first time—live music. Todd, having been to many sporting events, was accustomed to the flow of people, the flow of the crowd, the inning-by-inning segments that took place, but a whole new world was opened to him that night with Van Halen.

Show me a kid that has never lied in one fashion or another, and I will show you a kid that is lying. Everyone lies, especially teenagers, and Todd was no different. At the age of thirteen, Todd understood what a white-lie was compared to a full-fledged lie. Todd shared with me his scheme of all schemes to attend that concert. "My parents knew I was a Van Halen fan, but to get my parents to allow me to go, I told them that Jimmy's parents, Mike's parents, and Chris' parents were allowing them to go." Huge lie from Todd, but now really it was just a carrot dangling in front of his parents. It was up to them if they chose to take the bait. But a nibble or two was not enough for Todd's parents to say yes right off the bat, so he added a little more sugar to sweeten the pot. "They wouldn't let me go at first, so I told them Mr. Myres was chaperoning. They knew Mr. Myres well, just like all the parents, but it wasn't until I told them that Mr. Berger was going to be working the concert and that he promised to lookout for us, that they agreed to let me go." The little devil on Todd's should was revealed to me as he shared that memory. Ultimately, it worked. His half-truth made sense to his parents, and they agreed to let him go.

Perched from the rafters with a long-range sniper rifle is the vision I have of Mr. Berger guarding all of us kids, and Todd imagined the same sequence of events. In reality Mr. Berger was on the floor, working the backstage, hanging with the band—but Todd had to convince his parents otherwise, and it worked. Todd went on to tell me, "My dad and Skip were good friends, just like my dad and your dad—they were our coaches. That is what sold them, Mr. Berger working the concert." Trust is what Todd just described, and it is just as needed today as it was back in '84. Parents knew each other, and they knew each other well. There was a solid bond. Todd continued, "He (Skip) promised that he would check in on us, and that is what sold my parents on saying okay." Todd was laughing as he said this, because the little white-lie worked.

MTV was unbelievable back in the 80s, but there was something missing, they didn't play enough rock music, like Van Halen. Well, that stuff was not on all the time, and you had to time it just right to catch the 80s big-hair bands. Older teens and older siblings was how my classmates and I were introduced to Van Halen, before "*Jump*" was a thing. Todd told me who influenced him, "Mike Myres got me into Van Halen, because of his older brother (Jimmy). Mike said, you have got to listen to this stuff, so I did." That is how all of us boys welcomed Van Halen into our houses. It was Jimmy Myres, through his younger brother Mike, shedding light on the bands that we needed to listen to. "I was the oldest, with three younger sisters—I didn't have an older brother or sister to influence me, it was Mike Myres, through his older brother Jimmy, that influenced me." The grin on Todd's face expressed what the power of positive influence can do to warp a young mind...LOL...

Todd and I have some funny memories together, but the one that sticks out the most was our trip to Kings Island amusement park. It was so damn hot, that the lines were backed up for what seemed like miles, the sun was beating down on us both. His mom dropped us off at 10:00 am, and we zipped around the park catching a few rides. We were in line around high noon for the Viking Fury—this massive Viking ship that rocked from head to stern, mimicking a massive wave. One minute I was talking to Todd, I looked at the boat, then turned back, and Todd was gone—not far, but lying flat on his back on the asphalt. Todd had passed out. With that, the EMS, in their golf cart, whisked in and took Todd directly to the old German Village building, which had air-conditioning. They gave Todd some water, and he ate some ice cream. We laughed after we both knew Todd was fine. He hadn't eaten anything all day, so nothing like water and ice cream inside a beer village to cool off and comeback to life... I think we had a met or bratwurst to refuel us for the next wave...

Rock posters, we all had them up in the 80s—that is just what boys did, if it wasn't baseball or football posters—it was bands. Todd shared a hilarious story with me about the power of a poster— "I had an Iron Maiden poster in my room, only because the posters were cool at the time with the creature named Eddie. My grandma and grandpa would travel down from Cleveland, and they would sleep in my room. I got booted out. My grandma called my mom down, and she pointed out that somewhere on that poster was 666 in fine print—I had to take it down. Grandma and grandpa wanted nothing to do with rock, they enjoyed Pat Boone, Elvis, Brenda Lee, and Perry Como, no way in hell was Iron Maiden going to be welcomed into their lives."

Adventures with the family are always one for funny moments, Todd told me. "The minute I hear a Van Halen song on the radio, turn it up, that is the first thing I say. Then of course everyone in the car must be silent, so I can enjoy the song, sing along, and play my air-guitar solo." That is how it is with Todd, when he hears Van Halen—"Shut up! The band is on!" Todd went on to share a memory, "When I was driving with my grandparents in Cleveland, I used to spend a lot of time with them—We were on our way to see *Back to the Future,* me, and my sister Tonia. A Van Halen song comes on the radio, and I told Grandma to turn it up, and she said, 'That is too loud. You are going to hurt your ears.'" Todd in his chair, laughing with pure zest, his eyes glazed over, laughing so hard. However, Grandma did give him sound advice. And to this day, Todd does not wear hearing-aids...Great job meemaw.

"Growing up my parents had a ton of records, they were fans of The Doors, but music was not always on—it was not a big influence, talk radio was always on and the Reds. Music was not a big part of our household, no one played an instrument, other than us kids at IHM playing the recorder. Music as an influence, came from outside the home." Todd shared. The amazing conversation piece that Todd shared with me, was that his parents, as far as he knew, had never been to a concert and that he may have been the first one in his family to attend one, and Todd was only thirteen....

What amazed me while interviewing folks for this book, is how the brain gets stimulated. Visions of the past just pop right up upon hearing a word or two—we are taken back instantly to our youth. We reflect, we rejoice, we recollect, we laugh, we reminisce, and we reflect upon our emotions and our thoughts of what was taking place then, as we were about to leave grade school. Todd had a funny memory about our friends Mike Myres and Mark Zloba. "They were going to form a rock band in seventh grade called Broken Diamond. Their first album was going to be *Diamonds Broken*." Amazing that Todd could recall the band name, and the band's debut album title. That is the power of positive memories from our youth.

Today Todd is married to his wife Tosh and has four kids. Their oldest daughter is twenty-nine, and their three sons are twenty-four, twenty-two, and eighteen respectively. Todd is an operations manager for a major courier service here in Cincinnati—one that operates 24-hours a day, 365 days a year. His specialty is dealing with hospitals. So, you can imagine, the amount of stress that job entails—yet, speaking with Todd, showing his true colors today, as he did back in '84—Todd a happy, confident, daring, and outgoing. He told me he had ADHD in 7th grade, but all that proves to me is that Todd had an electric spunk to him, which carried over to his adult life as husband, father, and an elite businessman.

The Healthcare Worker

(Jimmy Myres)

"1984" Junior year photo

When we are young, all we want to be is older. We want to experience more, and we don't want to be tethered any longer—we want free reign, we want to feel independent, we want to be free, but moreover we don't want to feel like a kid any longer. We are always looking for the next outlet, going to a friend's house to spend the night, staying out after dark, staying up late, watching a rated "R" movie, and the feeling that you're not constantly being look at from afar. Binoculars are a great example, big bother always watching, parents always looking over our shoulders, that feeling becomes a very serious problem between twelve and thirteen years old.

When we are 9, we want to be 10 (Double Digits)
When we are 12, we want to be 13 (Teenager)
When we are 13, we want to be 16 (Driver's license)
When we are 16, we want to be 18 (High School Grad)
When we are 18, we want to be 21 (Drink alcohol legally)
When we are 21, we want to be 25 (Insurance goes down)

Then from twenty-five until fifty, that is when it really becomes surreal, that is the empty slot, the time when all the anticipation builds up, all the education pays off, our goals become reality, the bookends are filled with our to-do lists, marriage, kids, soccer-moms, baseball coaching—then it hits us at fifty, *AARP* sends us the notice in the mail. We finally hit the age, that we never thought we would hit, at the age of twelve.

All I wanted in life growing up was an older sibling, whether that would be a sister, so I could beat up and protect her from idiot boyfriends, or an older brother that I could run around with, be the third wheel, and experience life other than that of the first child. The first child is the guinea pig, kid gloves, extra baths, extra room child protection gear, extra layers of clothing, and rain boots. Parents walk outside with them, and don't allow them to leave their sight. Then comes the second child, everything we know about what to expect, when expecting, is thrown out the door. Parents become experts through trial and error, and the second child is the one who gets to cross the busiest street at a younger age, because the oldest sibling led the way. The first kid is the test object, and they were the sample container—then from the second to third to fourth kid, each one has a protective layer removed.

Jim Myres Jr—he was the coolest cool, without me even knowing who he was, other than he was Mike's older brother. He was the one with the driver's license and the one that was giving Mike all the ins and outs of rock & roll. Jim was the epitome of monkey see, monkey do, for he was the older brother that was so current on the music scene in high school. Mike picked up his lingo, his artistic creations, his rhythm, and his rhyme, and then Mike would then bring that vision back to grade school. Jim was in essence the line leader, he was testing the waters, and Mike was there with a very watchful eye.

Van Halen 1 and *Van Halen 2* were never heard of in my house, but in Jim's life, he was living in that world. *Diver Down* and *Fair Warning*, those were being played in Jim's room too, and Mike was right there to listen to them. *Women and Children First*, what is there a fire, are we evacuating the school????? That was my take on the album, and *Diver Down*, who was that guy to bring Jacque Cousteau into my life, having seen *2000 Leagues Under the Sea*—Kirk Douglas.

Jim was the older brother; he was the cool dude that my buddies and I saw through Mike's eyes. Jim was living and breathing everything that we wanted to be so badly at twelve-years-old. He was in high school; he was Greg Brady to us. He was the real spinal tap moment in high school looking back through twelve-year-old eyes. Mike was creating our world of VH because of Jim's positive influence on him, which then created a world of fire through the classroom. Van Halen was introduced to my buddies and me, because Mike would explain to us that we needed to listen to them, and that we needed to watch *MTV*. Jim, being a Bob Ross of his own kind, could draw the Van Halen logo, which then Mike mimicked, then we copied Mike and drew the VH logo on our book covers, which were brown paper bags.

When I would go over to Mike's house in grade school, Jim was nowhere to be found, our paths never crossed, for Jim was out and about. Going down to the basement and seeing Jim's room, now that was just so cool for a seventh grader. He didn't have a door to his room, he had beads that you would just walk through—talk about pure awesomeness. Then in his little, tiny bedroom, there were posters of all the rock bands, an impressive stereo system, and of course just a scene of what rock & roll was to the older guys. Jim was elite to me, having zero recollection of even what he looked like back then, he still influenced me. Jim was sharing his world with me, without even knowing it.

Here I am writing a book about all my buddies' first concert, and lo and behold, Jimmy tells me the story about his first concert. Guess who was there with him? You guessed it, his dad. "My first concert was with my dad. It was KISS. It was a family outing." I noticed right away what Jimmy expressed about the concert, "It was a family outing." I noted this earlier about Jimmy's dad... It was important for Mr. Myres to take his family. It was not a matter of maybe, or I will see if I can get off work. It was a mission that needed a platoon leader, and Mr. Myres took it upon himself to lead the troops. "I still have my tour book and my ticket stub, and those tickets were $9.00 dollars." The signature mark of any true fan, is still having the tour book and ticket stub. This KISS concert was a family outing. His dad was there, his two brothers were there, Dave and Mike—the Fab Four attended the KISS concert, and the memorabilia will mark that evening.

Teenagers will be teenagers, as the saying goes—but hanging out with friends, being in the moment is just as fun as being involved with a spectacle. That is where Jimmy's brain was the night of the Van Halen concert. He was with his friends, hanging out, being a rebel without a cause, thus then realizing, hey we are having fun, but we need to roll. "I never made it to the opening band—when Dad left to start picking you guys up, my ride was not even here yet. We had to do some pre-game activities and we had Little Kings Beer. We headed over to my buddy's house, shot pool for a bit, threw back a few cold ones, and played a little guitar. When I realized the time, oh crap we better get going. We made it in, right as Autograph was walking off the stage, and the lights came on." This was the mindset of Jimmy, the teenage rocker to a T—the importance of strumming the guitar leading up to a Van Halen concert, that feeling of music, the anticipation of seeing the band, and listening to the *1984* album on the stereo. Now that is cool, a band of brothers so to speak. Jimmy and his pals riffing, jamming, and trying to create a collage of music before the concert. Excitement had set in, heart racing, fingers flying down the neck of the guitar, back and forth. Jimmy was melding into Eddie, and his buddies were the band.

"That night in '84, I had nosebleed tickets—but me and my buddy Eric were sitting there, and he saw two guys get kicked out, which was second row up on the side of Michael Anthony—we weaseled our way down, and the usher stopped us." Jimmy chuckled as he remembered, "I told the usher, 'We will be cool.' The usher let us down." That is hard to do today, because ushers are guarding every single ticket price in every venue. If no one is in attendance, it's hard to weasel your way down to the field, a concert, or any outing—those tickets are outrageous. But Jimmy accomplished his goal, took advantage of a hoodlum, that probably Mr. Berger and his crew threw into the paddy wagon, thus making it safer for all us boys. Just like all the moms thought Mr. Berger would provide—a bodyguard.

"I was kind of in a high school band," Jimmy attested. "I played rhythm guitar. We didn't have a band name, but it was a great way to get the guys together, drink a little beer, and try to jam." Try to jam, just like the night leading up to the concert. Music is an outlet for Jimmy, a way to venture out of the real world, and put himself among the Rock Gods. It is everyone's dream to be in a band if you can play an instrument, and Jimmy's case was no different. Jimmy grew up with so many rock legends. *Guitar Hero* was not even created, yet Jimmy and his buddies were foreshadowing a future Christmas gift that millions of kids would receive in 2005.

Jimmy, jamming with his buds, in the early 80s.

"We could always play at Marty's house. We could play there till 10 p.m. on a school night. He lived right around the corner. It was hard to move his drum set, and his parents were so cool," Jimmy shared. S
"That night after the lights flipped on, a Van Halen pin was laying on the floor, I picked it up and took it home." To Jimmy, that night is marked

by a simple $5.00 pin—nothing flashy, nothing over the top, just a black pin with a Van Halen logo. That is Jimmy's piece of the concert. That's the story he can tell over and over. *Top Jimmy*, yes that song by Van Halen, would express Jimmy's night back in 1984. He was on top of the world.

Jimmy's Van Halen pin that he found on the floor that night back in 1984.

The Van

Mr. and Mrs. Myres' van—photo submitted by the Myres' family album.

Back in the early 80s vans only came in one size and were always seen as the getaway van in movies. There are two TV vans that will always standout to me. One is the Mystery Machine, with the gang from *Scooby-Doo* all in there, the light blue paint job and the flowers on the side. Groovy man. The second is *The A-Team* van, the black sleek looking van, all-terrain urban assault vehicle, with the red stripe through the middle of it, which led up to the red fin on the roof. But the van that is most important to me and brings back the best memories is the Myres' van.

When I think of a band, and a van, I think of the vehicle Dewy Fin had in the *School of Rock*—here is this wannabe teacher teaching young grade-school kids about the power of rock. He teaches them the value of understanding music, and how to open their hearts and their minds—to expand beyond just schoolwork. In the middle of the movie, they load up in his van, an old black beater with band stickers all over the back window to audition for the battle of the bands. The kids are all musically inclined, gifted in various classical genres, but it is Dewy that brings out their inner "core" to perform on stage. Here they all are piled up in his van, listening to rock tunes, and just having the time of their lives. Anxiety, blood pumping, heart racing with anticipation of performing live in front of a panel of judges. When I saw this movie for the first time, I could not stop thinking about all of us piled in Mr. Myres' van, traveling down the road in style to our first gig…. A van and a band just go together so well.

That baby blue, sleek looking vehicle was a must have for the Myres' family, eight kids, plus a soccer coach running the team around, and that night back in 1984, that van was our means of transportation. The Ford E series, known as the Econoline, was our slick ride that evening. How cool was that? My buddies and I were going to pile into this cool van for our evening at the Van Halen concert.

What was fun about this van, was the leg room, the row seating, and how you could walk from the back to the front to the middle and to the back again, without having to pull over to the side of the road. There was nothing aerodynamic about this hunking piece of equipment. By no means was this gas efficient, this was a pure gas guzzling machine, Michigan built, American made beast. In my mind, it was built for one reason and one reason only, to haul kids to the Van Halen concert.

This van had been a special part of my friends and my life for a long time. In grade school my class went away for a retreat weekend, everyone had to go. Lo and behold, Mrs. Myres (Barb) was our driver, for Mr. Myres was manning his battle station at the pharmacy. I got to sit in the front seat, no seat belt was required, and Mike and all of our classmates, about seven or eight of us were driven off to the retreat center.

I was aware of what a stick shift was, my dad had a Renault back in the 70s, with the shifter on the floor. This van was unique, because the shifter was on the column, three on the tree. Mrs. Myres was amazing! The memory of her driving that huge van, is a vision that stands out as vividly today, as if it were yesterday. Mrs. Myres had all of us guys in the van, bouncing around, and she is levelheaded, shifting the gears with ease. She was in control.

That night back in '84, we were jacked up, pumped up, and talking amongst ourselves. I remember the conversation; we were playfully arguing about whether Eddie was going to play the keyboards or the guitar during the song *Jump*. We volleyed back and forth saying things like, "Will there will be a stand-in for him at the keyboards?" or, "No way, Eddie cannot play Frankenstein on that song." And, "So maybe they will drop out the keyboards and just play the electric guitar."

Looking five steps ahead is what business experts always say, not just the next step, but five steps away. In that van we were playing out the next five steps and creating a scenario. We were imagining the jam set in our brains, as if we had telepathy and could tell Eddie, "Please only play the guitar." Well, we were all right. Eddie did play the keyboards to the song *1984*, which then led into him only playing the guitar in the song *Jump*—it never mattered to us either way.

The conversation in that van must have been mind boggling to our chauffer, Mr. Myres. If I had been a fly on the wall, I know I would have died from laughter hearing all the scenarios being created by us kids. But that is what kids do, they are playful, with not a care in the world, except for the guitar situation during *Jump*. That was all we were worried about.

Here we are in 2024, and everyone is driving SUVs. Everywhere you look, they seem to be all over the place. Every once in a while, I will catch sight of a Ford E series van, and the minute my eyes are locked in, my memory of Van Halen kicks in instantly. It was a special van, it was a special night, but what made it extra special was we were shuttled to Cincinnati Gardens to witness Van Halen's magic, and be welcomed into Van Halen's world of rock 'n' roll.

Eventually the van had to be put down. Not to put words into the Myres family's mouth, but the day the van made its last spin around Cincinnati, I believe was a sad day—not in terms of crying, but in terms of the memories that van created with their family. Eight kids grew up in that special vehicle, and I know they got their money's worth.

Like Van Halen being the perfect band, back in 1961 Ford's van designers had a vision of the perfect van when they developed the E series. They possibly envisioned families taking road trips, camping, car-pooling, coaches hauling kids and sports equipment, and maybe even plumbers using this vehicle. Van Halen, way back before the *Van Halen 1* album was created, they too had a vision of one day kids of all ages coming to watch them play. The Van and Van Halen will always be tied together for me. So, the next time you see a vehicle that brings back memories, tell your spouse about it, tell your kids about it, and share that positive memory. Perhaps, allow them to see a side of you that you have never expressed before. Believe me, people love to hear stories, because their brains will be spinning to tell you their story, that's just how it goes—unless you are with a zipped-lipped person, which doesn't happen to often on a road trip.

"You're gonna need a bigger boat." A classic line from the movie *Jaws*. And, that was Mr. Myres' mentality when dealing with the van. We need more rows, we need to handle more passengers, and we have a family of eight kids, so yes, we are going to need more seats. "We had an extra row of seats made for the van," Mr. Myres said. "Ford would not allow an extra row of seats, some violation at the time—only allowed so many rows, so I had a row created by a guy north of Cincinnati, up in Mason. They looked the same, felt the same, and it was an excellent addition to the van." Overcome and adapt, two words that described the mindset of Mr. Myres. He had the biggest van, but he needed more seats—so what did he do? He created his own.... Genius.

Once Mr. Myres modified the van, he explained, "I could fit twenty kids in that van. If I can fit five kids in my Fiat X 1/9, then loading up that van beyond capacity was no issue." According to the seating capacity of a Ford E150 today, it has a cargo space of 236.5 cubic feet, and as a passenger van can seat up to eight passengers. Back in 1984, you certainly got more bang for your buck, because there were no seatbelt rules in the state of Ohio, the more the merrier. That night with all us guys loaded up in the van was a special occasion. It was our limo taking us to the concert, and we were rolling in style. We had so much space to laugh and sing Van Halen tunes. We were not bunched up; we were not sardines. We were four guys sprawled out in this massive vehicle, a monster of a truck, to put it lightly.

When you make a car purchase, you think that you will be unique and the soul wheels on the road. However, once you roll off the lot, and drive down the highway, you realize that everyone and their grandma owns the same car in the same color. It's weird the way this works, but it works every single time, and it's probably happened to you. It was no different for Mr. Myres, and he admitted, "That blue van was everywhere."

Like anything that is in the family for a long period of time, such as a car or truck, or in this case a van, it is a part of the family. The Myres' van created memories for not only for them, but for my buddies and me as well. We love our cars—we wash them, bathe them, check the oil, change the tires, clean the windows. This special piece of metal truly is an important member of the family and is a huge part of memorable stories and numerous outings. In speaking with Jimmy Myres about the van, he shared a fun tidbit about what he remembered, "Vacations and smelly shoes—our feet stunk so badly. My dad took our gym shoes and hid them in the engine compartment, so that none of us could smell those shoes." Road Trip!!!!!! All of us have blared those words at one time or another. Who doesn't love to get in the car and head for a destination? Now, just imagine the Myres family, eight kids all piled in there with their dog Fred, a gym locker atmosphere to a T. So, like any good sailor, having been confined on a smelly ship, Mr. Myres knew what to do, handled it well, and took charge.

The Ford had a unique shifting assembly, known as "three on the tree," which means it had a three-speed manual transmission with the gearshift mounted on the steering column. One was down, two was up and to the right, and three was straight down. Reverse was up and to the top left, and of course neutral was in the middle. This required a clutch as well. This massive tank was truly one that was battle tested yet, was so difficult to maneuver. I can only imagine get away drivers trying to use this, they probably always got caught....it is hard. "Three on the tree column—I never mastered driving that," Jimmy told me. Yet his mom Barb, on the other, had was like a formula one driver. "My mom could drive that van like a bus," Jimmy smirked as he recalled his mom driving.

Leases were not big back in the 70s and 80s, purchasing a vehicle meant you were going to drive it till the cows came home. Jimmy puts it into words, "He drove that thing until the wheels fell off." No one was getting a car every two years; no one was getting a car every three years. You drove off the lot with the intention of reaching 100,000 miles and then some, before even thinking about looking at the Sunday ads for vehicles. No way, José. You get what you can afford, and you enjoy this fine piece of Detroit auto for a long as possible.

All the guys that night remember the van, and Todd was no different. He shared his memory, "I have told the story about the van ride numerous times. I remember folks in that van were pissed at me, I can recall that vividly." Todd goes on, "I did not shut up; I had a big mouth. I was ADHD, and only two things kept me in check, running around with sports and focusing on something important. Before the van ride, I had snuck and watched Eddie Murphy's *Delirious*. I recited the whole thing in that van ride. Mr. Myres just wanted me to shut up." Todd and I laughed so hard in my dining room, as he shared this memory with me. "I repeated *Delirious* word for word and said words that us good Catholic boys should not have been saying, but hey we were off to see Van Halen. I was so excited about the concert, that I felt I needed to share what Eddie Murphy had taught me, with the whole van load of my buddies."

Sneaking a peek at a rated "R" movie and going to see Van Halen at the age of thirteen, it was apparent that we were becoming men. The van ride was just another indicator that we wanted to be older. We wanted to be in the NOW. We were not babies any longer—Eddie, David, Michael and Alex, they were the NOW, and our drive over to the Gardens proved to me, that the age of innocence was about to be washed away. Todd reciting Eddie Murphy was classic. Cuss words, sentence enhancers, sprinkle on a few to heighten the point—either way, if you want to talk like a sailor, then you are going to have to work like a sailor. After high school Todd indeed did enlist in the Navy. Todd, had one step-up on his shipmates, thanks to *Delirious* and the Van Halen concert. Proof that was justified in him defending our country—Todd, I salute you, and thank you for your service.

"The Van!!!" Mike roared to me as I asked him about the get-away vehicle. Which I am sure was ideal for any bank robberies, quick in and out, of course with the right driver. Mike saw it a different way, "It was the church van." His family was big on church, which just so happened to be attached to our grade school. The E series van was always at the ready, with Mike being thirteen in '84, he was nearly ready to start driving the beast within a few years "I could not drive that van," Mike revealed. In his defense, that would have been very difficult to attempt under a learner's permit.

Deep-sixed—the van officially hit E.....End of Life. Gone but not forgotten. Like everything we own, something that is tangible, something that is bought, with a very limited life span is gone. Now we only have memories of those items, which we once possessed. We move on to something new, something fresh—yet still not forgetting the excellent times we had with it. Memories were created, and stories can still be shared. Pictures of the Myres' special van can still be seen, but they can't walk out to the driveway, and catch one last glimpse of her. That will never happen again. We said good-bye to something that provided more than transportation. We said good-bye to a van that gave the Myres family and my buddies terrific excursions, journeys and memories. The van will forever be a part of the family, and will be recalled every time Van Halen is played...

Cincinnati Gardens

Hockey, Boxing and Basketball—this piece of art was set in the brick walls of the Gardens, to the left and right of the main entrance. Thus,

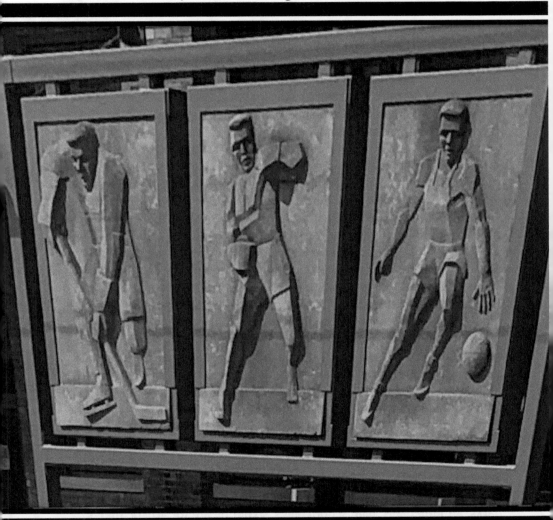

explaining the vision of the architect, sports.
(Picture taken by Jim Serger at the Sign Museum, in Cincinnati, Ohio)

I have been blessed to have attended so many awesome venues sprouting up as youngster. Riverfront Stadium, the home to the Big Red Machine, I saw the greats such as Joe Morgan, Johnny Bench and of course my favorite Pete Rose. My household consisted of a sports atmosphere almost 365 days a year, with the exception being Christmas morning. If the sun was out, I was tossing ball with Dad, or I would drag my brother out to shoot hoops down at the corner. Riverfront Stadium also housed the Cincinnati Bengals, so growing up and watching them too was an absolute thrill. Ken Anderson, Anthony Muñoz, and Cris Collinsworth were household names. Baseball and football were not the only games in town, Xavier University basketball was extensive and University of Cincinnati basketball was massive. Oscar Robinson was an enormous Cincy icon, having played on the Cincinnati Bearcats and the pro team, the Cincinnati Royals.

My mom had zero athletic ability, and when I say zero, I mean zero, however my mom was a master thespian. She loved plays, theatre, musicals and of course ice skating, so I knew who Dorothy Hamill was long before my buddies did. I was aware of *Bye Bye Birdie*, *Gone with the Wind*, ABBA, and disco all because of my mom. She was the left-brainer in the family, and her creativity was always on point. Mom could sew, paint, build a bird house, cook salmon loaf to perfection and hang wallpaper with the best. Her skill set for performing was something I had grown accustomed to. Mom and Dad would always go to the movies, and they loved seeing and attending live performances. So having grown up in the late 70s and 80s, Ringling Brothers Barnum & Bailey Circus was always on our radar, and sure enough Dad would get us box tickets and we all would go as a family. Grandma and Grandpa on my dad's side would often join us too. My brother and I were seeing live performances, going to the Ice Capades, and hitting up the rotating attractions at Riverfront Coliseum, which sat adjacent to Riverfront Stadium.

Mom also communicated that there was more to life than sports, and she made sure that my dad, brother and I got to venture off into her love and passion, the fine arts. Mom loved to watch ice skating. She was just in awe of it, so Dad always found a way to make sure that Mom's love of the arts was continually streaming in our life. Mom took us to the festivals, parks, antique malls, high school plays, so her desire for artistic things was nurtured and fulfilled. She was fond of sports, because she got to root for us, see us in action, and of course gossip with all her lady friends on the sidelines. She loved hanging out with the other moms, and a good time was had by all.

But Cincinnati Gardens, well that was one arena that Mom and Dad had the fondest of memories growing up as kids. It was located on the northeast side of Cincinnati, Ohio, located at 2250 Seymour Avenue in Bond Hill. That was their hot spot. The doors swung open on this arena on February 22, 1947, when my mom and dad were one and one and a half years old respectively. The surface was concrete with an ice floor built right over it, which would accommodate the AHL/IHL Cincinnati Mohawks hockey team from 1949-1958. Xavier University played basketball there from 1949-1979, then again from 1983-2000. Of course, there was Mom and Dad's alma mater, the Cincinnati Bearcats who played hoops there from 1949-1954, then again from 1987-1989. The one team that Dad always talked about was the Cincinnati Royals (NBA) who played there from 1952-1972 and was the team of Oscar Robinson. I mean this place was booming with activity for kids and adults in the Cincinnati area, and guess what? My parents and all their friends were right there experiencing this amazing venue.

When Cincinnati Gardens first opened it could house 11,000 people at full capacity. Now with my parents born in 47' and 48', they grew right with this amazing building, along with their parents. That is what my parents shared with me, long before I knew what an arena, venue, stadium, or coliseum was even about. My parents, for entertainment, were going to the Cincinnati Gardens to bear witness to the stars. Ice skating is not as popular in Cincinnati today, as it was way back when. In the 60s, Dad and Mom would go to the Gardens to ice skate indoors, although they learned how to ice skate outdoors. It seemed as if Mom would point out to me every single pond or reservoir throughout Cincinnati that Dad and she skated on. At some point I believe she even said that she skated on the Ohio River, when it froze over, back in 1979. I call BS on that. The Gardens was also the home to the Cincinnati Wings (CPHL) 1963-1964, Cincinnati Swords (AHL) 1971-1974, and home to the Cincinnati Slammers (CBA) 1984-1987. This place was a-rocking, so don't bother knocking...come on in, almost any given day, my parents, their friends, their parents could watch a winter sport live, or even participate after hours on the rink.

Sign Museum in Cincinnati, Ohio—picture taken by Jim Serger. All that remains of this once impressive arena, is CINCINNATI GARDEN—for the S is missing.

Sports fulfilled my dad's needs, Mom's too. Ice skating, now that was what Mom loved. She enjoyed the skill and the grace of the figure eight. She knew that took brains, concentration, and skills that tough guy sports never offered, and that's why she loved it. Boxing well, she never liked that at all, but hey boxing events were even housed at the Cincinnati Gardens. Legendary boxer and hall-of-famer Ezzard Charles had a heavyweight fight there in 1949. The Gardens were at full capacity, with 11,000 fans watching him defeat Joey Maxim, just one week after the arena opened. The Gardens even had roller derby and was home to Cincinnati Rollergirls and the Cincinnati Jolters in 1971. I think my mom and dad went to one, too rough for mom's blood so they never returned.

But the main event at Cincinnati Gardens was the concerts. Good old-fashioned rock 'n' roll, and huge names headlined on that stage. My parents and grandparents were there and had the opportunity to see such greats as The Crickets, Fats Domino, Chuck Berry, Lavern Baker, Jerry Lee Lewis, Frankie Lymon and The Chantelles. In August of 1964, the biggest musical act of the time came to The Gardens, The Beatles. The Fab Four were in Cincinnati, and everyone who was cool, hip, and in was there to see them firsthand—but that was a hard ticket to get, just ask my mother-in-law. She opted not to buy a ticket, but waited by the stage door with her friend, to watch the boys exit to their waiting car, and proceeded to chase them around town, finally arriving at what they thought was their hotel, which it wasn't. Sadly, she never met the band. Cincinnatians had one night and one night only to see the boys from Liverpool. There were many other huge artists that played at the Gardens stage including: The Rolling Stones (1965), The Supremes (1968), The Jackson 5 (1970 & 1971), Elvis Presley (1971 and 1973), The Grateful Dead (1973), and many others. this arena was the hottest ticket in town for many, many, years. But the one that stood out for me, was Van Halen on March 9, 1984. That was the biggest event that I had ever been to, one that I could connect with my parents, one that I knew would stand the test of time, for I thought as a youngster that the Gardens would last forever.

In March of 2018, Cincinnati Gardens was torn down, left a vacated field. What was once powerful and sought after, was now just a piece of history only in our minds. Not a glimmer of any structure remains, it is a has been. The memories created in that structure go back many generations for moms, dads, and teenagers. People had their first dates, first concerts, first basketball games, first hockey games, and even learned how to ice skate at Cincinnati Gardens. Unfortunately, it is gone now, but like anything worth sharing Cincinnati Gardens gave me the best memories as a young man. The Gardens is still alive in my heart and brain as it was to my friends and me forty years ago. Its memory lives on.

I was sad the day I heard that the Gardens was demolished. It was a piece of my boyhood that was wiped off the face of the earth. That 19-acre piece of property will now be logged in the history books as one of the greatest sites ever erected in the Midwest, for when it was built back in 1949, it was the seventh largest indoor arena in the United States. The seats were so tiny, it was so cramped in there, that even at a hockey game, just a t-shirt was good enough, the humidity level was so high, you could see the fog seeping through the hardwood floors on some nights. The Gardens was where I saw the Cincinnati Cyclones play in the 90s, as well as the Mighty Ducks. But Van Halen, who played two nights there, March 8th and 9th, will always be remembered by me, passed down to my daughter through my stories, as well as talked about at Thanksgiving and at Christmas. The whole Serger, Berger, Myres, and Zimmerman families have been and will always have ties to that magnificent arena. No one can take those memories away from us. They are protected, sacred, and preserved forever. Long after this book is out, generation after generation will have heard a story or two about what Cincinnati Gardens gave to so many young ladies and young men. The power to savor the moment will flourish onto others.

"It was a sad day, there is a big part of my memory that is gone, my past. I still think they could have done something with that location," Skip shared. "I saw The Beatles at the Gardens. I watched basketball games, 4x4 monster truck shows, and hockey with my wife and kids. The Gardens created so many memories. I saw Dusty Springfield in concert and took the kids to the circus. It was a great location, great venue, you could get close to everything. It was sad the day they tore down the Gardens." Skip continued, "I used to work all the traffic details for all of the events they used to have, and I even ice skated there too."

A monumental piece of art was located in Bond Hill, Ohio—something that truly was a part of so many who lived in the greater Cincinnati area. It was not only for concerts, but for youth activities, the doors always seemed open to the public. People could shoot some hoops after hours or play hockey there like my dad did in college, but the one big ticket item for love birds, was ice skating. Date night was prevalent back in the 60s as it is today. Couples have always sought out memorable experiences, fun activities, and exhilarating events. Mr. Myres shared, "I had been going there since grade school and remember ice skating there. I was good at one foot skating, hands on the railing, in other words, I was awful." Awful, well that explains it well. He overcame his fear, stood like a flamingo, and even attempted to do his Scott Hamilton routine. It was not the Olympic tryouts, but it was an outing that Mr. Myres could do in his youth. Like all good things, time caught up with the Gardens, and as Bob Dylan sang, "The Times They Are a-Changin."

Buildings back then were literally built to withstand the test of time, tornadoes, hurricanes or even earthquakes. The Gardens is historical in so many avenues, Beatles played there, Elvis played there, hockey was played, basketball was played and of course ice-skating. But as time went on the college programs were able to build their own arenas, pro teams came and went, the only thing keeping the Gardens alive were, the Cincinnati Cyclones—but it was hard to compete with other new establishments. The biggest one was Riverbend Music Center, which was built the same year of our 1984 concert. It is on the Ohio River, about five miles east of downtown Cincinnati, and it was built with an outdoor theme, open air concept, and it housed 20,500 paying customers. Nearly 10,000 more than the Gardens could hold. Needless to say, the Gardens was now in direct competition with Riverbend and Riverfront Coliseum, which was indoor facility in Downtown Cincy, that housed 17,500 patrons.

When you grow up with a piece of the community, it is very easy to say, stay open. Mr. Myres put it softly, "It was a solid ass building, they could have done something with it." Yes, use it for something else, but what? Competition was fierce, folks Mr. Myers' and Mr. Berger's age, that were once teenagers attending the Gardens, now had families. They were not venturing over there as frequently. The community folks who lived near Bond Hill were now empty nesters, or grandmas and grandpas. Their focus had shifted with age, they were now attending grandkids games and their school activities. Reaching the masses like it once did, was gone. Generation X was passing levees, passing new zoning laws, and reaching out for bigger and better outlets, not the old historical ones, but brand-new shiny things.

As we look back, memories are all we have now, and of course an empty lot. One memory that Mr. Myres shared with me was, "I went to a Harlem Globetrotter game there, where only a handful of people can say, the Kings won. Everybody was pissed. They got their asses kicked that night." Very funny, everyone knows the Globetrotters will win upon entering the match-up, but that night, he got to see something unusual. Something off-the-cuff. The Globetrotters could be beat, and he was in attendance that night. He can attest that he was there to bear witness to this anomaly.

To be at Van Halen in the seventh grade with your dad at the Gardens is one thing, to be dropped off at the Gardens in eighth grade is a whole different thing. Mike shared with me that coming-of-age moment, when his dad began to trust him to be on his own. "My dad dropped me and a buddy of mine off at the Gardens. We saw Ratt, and Bon Jovi was the warmup band—we went by ourselves," Mike said. Then he went on, "Can you believe that? Two eighth graders at a concert by themselves, no way I would I do that today." Mike explained with a huge worried look on his face. The Gardens gave Mike his transformation, and today that building is demolished, six feet under, gone, a has been. Yet, Mike can still recall positive moments that the structure gave him, not only concerts, but hockey and the circus too. He remembers family outings and has great memories of attending numerous events with his friends. Gone, but not forgotten.

How many birthday parties were planned at the Gardens? Circus, sporting events, and of course concerts—all reasons to throw the kids in the van, see something at the Gardens, leave a mess for someone else to clean up, and acquire a positive memory for a day of celebration. That is what happened to Jimmy on his twenty-first birthday. He and his wife Lesa got to see Iron Maiden and Megadeth at the Gardens. Twenty-first birthday, now legal to down a cold one, no more sneaking it. Jimmy could stand there with a brewski and listen to *Run to the Hills.* For the record, anytime someone says I am turning twenty-one, or has a kid turning twenty-one, Jimmy will always remember who he was with, where he was, and what concert he attended. The Gardens gave him that memory, which is the key word, and Jimmy has that image logged in his memory banks for eternity.

Being four years older can make all the difference in the world, and for Jimmy Myres that was true. "I had been to at least fifteen to twenty concerts at the Gardens. I can remember parking in the gravel parking lot, walking in with beer in my hands." He was seventeen years old that night in 1984. He had his driver's license, and being a rocker, Jimmy sought out and attended many concerts at the older, historical venues in the Cincinnati area. "It was nostalgic," Jimmy added in expressing his take on the Gardens being knocked down. "A piece of him was removed that day," he went on to explain to me. The outings, the games, the concerts are now locked away in his personal vault, like millions of folks throughout greater Cincinnati—but Jimmy has something that nobody else, I would say, has...

"Van Halen left the stage, a few minutes later the encore came on. We were standing on our seats, fist bumping, high-fiving, screaming like crazy—suddenly, my leg went to the floor, and I was like what the hell happened? My seat broke. I picked up part of it and shoved it in my Army jacket. It was mine now." Jimmy gloated as he remembered that moment and continued. "That piece sits at my bar today." We all love talking points, and even build power-point slides to drive our message home. Jimmy has no reason to create a slideshow, because he has a sacred piece of the nostalgic building in his home. A picture is worth a thousand words—and Jimmy's piece of art, is an example of what the night meant to him. It's one thing to see Van Halen live, but it's a whole other thing to physically own a piece of the building, to commemorate the night. "Who else has a piece of their seat from the Cincinnati Gardens, which is not there anymore, from a Van Halen concert back in 1984? NO ONE, BUT ME!" People today buy a brick to memorialize an event or purchase a small placard to mark the special date, or circumstance. Jimmy literally has a piece of the crumbled building, and it is one heck of a talking piece—this wooden back, from a seat just rows away from Michael Anthony jamming on his bass—now that is a cool story.

"Sorry folks, park's closed." John Candy famously said in the classic movie *Vacation*. It's a great quote and puts into perspective that Cincinnati Gardens is closed, closed for good—o more outings. Things were changing, Todd explained it best, "It was a bummer, the day it closed—but concerts switched from indoor arenas to mega outdoor amphitheaters."

In interviewing Todd, Chris, Mike, and Jimmy as well as the dads, one thing is clear as day, the family outings were and are vividly remembered. Chris at the Van Halen concert, Jimmy at the Cyclones games, Todd at the Xavier games, Mr. Berger with The Beatles, Mike at the Ratt concert, and Mr. Myres with the Globetrotters. And for me, an outing to see Autograph open for Van Halen. I can still remember them running out on stage, which lead into their opening song, *Eruption*. Thank you Cincinnati Gardens for giving us memories that will last forever, thank you for allowing us to be a part of your life. You gave so much, and WE ALL THANK YOU!

Jimmy Myres' seatback, from Cincinnati Gardens.

Jimmy Myres' seatback from Cincinnati Gardens—clearly marked, to signify the evening with friends, and the monstruous evening with Van Halen.

Friendship

I read an interesting book last year called, *Who Will Cry When You Die*, written by Robin Sharma. In his book, Sharma goes through numerous points about how to create a life worth dying for, the impact you can have on others, the impact you can have on a family, the impact you can have with strangers, and the impact you can have on a community. He expresses that we are given one shot at this life, so make it count. So that when you die, people will want to come to your funeral, because you had an impact on their life in one fashion or another.

That is what this book is about. At its core, it is about four rockers that created a powerful concert experience, and because of that people flocked to see them. Fans wanted to listen to them and be in their presence. Watching Van Halen smile, *JUMP*, jam, well that was pure entertainment, and they give people their money's worth. The camaraderie between them seemed real, authentic, and one that would last forever. In my eyes, they were unstoppable, and still are to this day.

People come and people go in our lives all the time. I was sad when David Lee Roth left the band, because to me the band was now incomplete. Sure, I still bought into Van Hagar, sure I still bought their CDs—but to me, the band needed to get back together. I saw as friends, and friendship never dies. Sometimes it fades away, but like a boomerang, it always, if thrown correctly, will come back. That's pure friendship. The unconditional love for someone, sure there may be a few scars, a few years lost, or a few decades lost—but what is not lost is the absolute connection to a friend.

Van Halen produced "forever friends" that night in Cincinnati, and no one can take that away from us. When I see Mike at a high school reunion, he and I are still connected because of that concert. When I see Chris at the store, he and I are still connected because of that concert, as well as Todd, seeing his last name on the building in Cincinnati—Zimmerman, we are connected—blood brothers forever.

Fraternity life is something I was a part of in college as a Delta Tau Delta—but in grade school I joined an elite frat house, that being Van Halen, that night. We were around beer, girls, a major rock band. The lights were low, and we heard cussing, and we were surrounded by flames from lighters. We were "the animals," from *Animal House* that night. Sure, we were not old enough to do anything, but we were part of the crowd. Friendship is the epicenter of life, and it is what keeps us alive and well.

Sleepovers are a poignant reminder of our youth; it seems as if back in the 70s and 80s that's all my friends did—one weekend after another. On one occasion, that everyone seems to remember, we had a mammoth sleepover at Todd's house in his cool basement, which I already described. In speaking with Mike, he shared his crystal-clear memory, "My first taste of beer was at Todd's house, when he had the massive sleepover. We were standing in his dad's garage, with a fridge of cold ones. I grabbed a Stroh's. Popped it. Took a few sips. YUCK!!!" All us kids wanted to be older, we were trying everything in our power to feel and experience what older meant, and Mike was welcomed in with a taste palette full of YUCK!!!

Speaking with Todd about friendship, he delved right into how important it was to experience his first concert with his friends, and how he would like to get the old gang back together. He suggested, "Let's all meet up at Summit Elementary and throw together a baseball game." Mike chimed in, "When I think of the guys, I think of IHM baseball. And when I think of Chris, Todd, and Jimmy, I think of baseball and Van Halen." Baseball and Van Halen. Damn good combination to rattle off, when thinking about friends. That is how it is, how it was, and how it will always be. Todd went on to say, "I have forgotten a lot of things these past forty years, but there is still a ton I remember. We were all friends, we were teammates, we were classmates, we did everything together, and Van Halen was a part of that journey."

Our community here in Cincinnati is a big community—tons of subdivisions, schools, roads, malls, and of course Tire Discounters—seems they are at every stoplight. It's one thing to say you lived by someone growing up as a kid, but however Todd takes one step further, "Mike's kids and my kids are friends, and I owned a house right down the street from Mr. and Mrs. Myres, so I would see Mike pretty regularly." A hop, skip and a jump away from his youth. As an adult Todd was still close to Mike since they were practically neighbors. He was also close to Chris because they were lucky enough to work together. "Chris and I worked at Quikrete for a few years together." Quikrete is a company that specializes in loose concrete, and when you add water, it creates a solid bond. That is the perfect description of our friendship. We are still bonded forty years later.

IHM Baseball
Top left: Coach Gary Pierson and Todd Zimmerman
Middle: Jim Serger and Mike Myres
Bottom: Dave Myres and Tom Pieples

IHM Basketball
Top: Jim Serger, Todd Zimmerman, and Tom Pieples
Bottom: Chris Berger

Notice my number is #11, but it has no school name.
Notice Chris' jersey has our school's name, and he is #1—which was
originally #11. His mom, Jan, removed the other 1, which is why the 1 is
way off to our right.

In the early 80s moms had to be creative—Jan was one of the best.

"The friends that leave you feeling more alive after you're with them are magic in human form."

Cory Allen

Van Halen

It was 1984, and I was thirteen, and I was about to see the hottest band in the world with my buddies. The 1984 tour kicked off on January 18th in Jacksonville, Florida at Jacksonville Coliseum and would end on September 2nd in Nuremberg, Germany at Städtisches Station. As a kid, the simple fact that Van Halen was rolling through your small town was huge to me. I thought they would go to big towns like New York, Los Angeles, Miami, Chicago—those were the tour stops for massive bands. We are just small little Cincinnati. At the time I was aware that bands or huge events took place in other cities. They either played the west coast or the east coast, but not fly over country. I mean there really are only five cities in America, NY, Chicago, L.A., Miami and fly over country. Why would VH stop by my river city? Was it for the cheese coneys, or the five-ways from Skyline Chili? I got it, Hudy Delight beer, I mean we are a beer town, or just maybe it was because we sell brats and mets. Why else would they come here? Ultimately it doesn't matter, they played in Cincinnati for two nights, Thursday March 8th, and Friday March 9th—two concerts here in the Queen City. As a kid I didn't get it, but today I release Cincinnati was a sought-after town. We have northern Kentucky right across the Ohio River, to the west we have southeast Indiana—so three states can be drawn into the Cincinnati region very quickly, because they are less than thirty minutes away from each other. I think that's maybe why we got two nights when Nashville, Pittsburgh, Las Vegas, Austin, San Antonio only had one. That was very powerful, that Cincy could draw from Dayton, Columbus, Morgantown, Indianapolis, Louisville, and Lexington—the producers knew what they were doing when they put city lineup together.

I was the oldest kid in my family, rock 'n' roll wasn't a big deal in my household. We didn't talk about it too much. My parents spoke of the Beatles playing at Crosley Field (Cincinnati Reds home, 1912-1970) in 1965, but very, very rarely would we gab about rock bands making their way through Cincinnati, or Ohio for that matter. We talked about sports in school, while driving to games, or going to church. We had the family over on the weekends, which allowed us to visit with our aunts and uncles and Grandma and Grandpa. Before *Jump*, the Van Halen concert was not even on my radar. All of that changed when *Jump* came out. My feelings about rock changed and Van Halen is the reason. I wasn't into heavy metal. I wasn't into devil worshiping, or even the thought of how bands and anti-Christ were affiliated, but that was the message being pushed across the air waves. In my parent's eyes the album covers were explicit. Some had 666 on them, or the devil, or a cross. Most of them had guys standing around in black leather jackets—There was no way in hell my parents would allow me to see Ozzy, Iron Maiden or Judas Priest—no way, so why even bring it up.

Then *MTV* came along, with the 80s outfits, big hair, Aqua Net hair spray, bright colors, and cool looking rockers jumping around the screen. It seemed to me they were having a great time, smiling, and pumping out this jamming sound. With all of that, Van Halen was welcomed into our household. I mentioned earlier that I knew Mom had a thing for the band. They all were young, close to Mom's age in '84, and they were entertaining, cool, and fun, yet still took their work seriously. Alex Van Halen was thirty-one, David Lee Roth was thirty, Michael Anthony was thirty, and Eddie Van Halen was the baby at twenty-nine. My mom was thirty-six and my dad was thirty-seven, so Van Halen was young to them, but only slightly. My mom knew Eddie best because she was a fan of Valerie Bertinelli. She wasn't the only one, every boy I knew was a super fan of hers. She was cute, and I think the girls in my school were aware of Eddie and Valerie because of *Teen Beat* Magazine.

Sitting at his bar, down in the mancave of Chris' house, I pulled a fast one on him—the first question I asked him was, "1984, what is the first thing that comes to your mind when you hear that year?" "The cover of the album, of the kid smoking a cigarette." Chris exhaled his laughter. "I think of that cover, it is vivid in my memory. It means I have a devil inside of me, but I am still a good kid. I remember showing my mom that album cover. She said, 'It was so cute.' Then her voice changed, and said, 'OH MY GOD!!! He is smoking a cigarette.' 'Maybe it's a candy cigarette.'" I said back to her, innocently. With the good angel on his shoulder helping to guide him...

Chris continued, "Sundays after church my family would be home by the time Casey Kasem's Top 40 came be on, and my brother Scott and I would listen to the top 40. We would scrap about who is better, Michael Jackson or Van Halen. My brother was two years younger than me and was a huge Michael Jackson fan. I was the Van Halen fan. I would tell him, 'You have got to like Van Halen and not Michael Jackson.' I remember my brother walking around with a peanut butter and jelly sandwich like a king telling me Michael Jackson was number one for the week, and the following week Van Halen was number one, and so I was the hit of the household." Chris described in detail the morning when *Jump* went to #1— "I think Michael Jackson had been #1 for almost seven straight weeks, and *Jump* was #2, then it finally happened. Casey Kasem said, 'Slipping out of the top spot,' and I knew right away that *Jump* was the #1 song in the land." Chris stated, as he was standing at his bar, with a huge smile on his face and raising a glass of bourbon to the rock gods. In your face Scotty—but in a nicer way.

Beat It was a massive hit for Michael Jackson, but to me it took Eddie's guitar solo to put that into the #1 slot—Scotty and Chris had to be thrilled to hear they collaborated on a song together. Eddie to me made that song go to #1, I am sure tons of folks on the other side will argue, which is fine—but I think that a great song, to be an awesome song needs a little pizzaz, and that's what Eddie added to the tune.

It is special to see a father and son bond. Baseball, golf, watching The Masters—or even just going out back to have a catch. But in 1984, Skip and Chris were given the ultimate experience, the experience of seeing Chris' favorite rock band, and meeting them in person. No one can take that moment away from them. Van Halen not only delivered one hell of a concert but gave Skip and Chris the glue that melded their relationship tighter and stronger. Forty-years later they still have the ultimate story to rehash and share together.

"One of the most exciting nights my son ever had," Skip Berger explained as to what Van Halen means to him. "I was so excited to be a part of that." Skip went on further, "It was an exciting time for Chris, and it meant a lot to me." To Skip, It was just a concert, it was part of his job, it paid the bills and put food on the table—that was the mindset of Skip forty years ago, that night March 7th, 1984—on Wednesday night, leading into his normal beat on Thursday morning—nothing new to report, same police car, same uniform, same hours, same lunch spot—but something over the horizon was about to happen to him and his son, as well as all us buddies—we were about to be introduced to Van Halen, figuratively and literally. Skip was hands-on, and we were in row ten.

"I have worked many details for folks that were famous, and folks that thought they were famous, and they treat you like garbage. Van Halen made you feel a part of what they were doing. They treated you with respect, they treated me and my fellow cops the way we were treating them—with respect," Skip said.

RESPECT! Aretha would be so, so, so, happy to hear this—forty years ago, and the powerful word that Skip describes Van Halen with, is respect. A powerful word to describe a rock band, and to still have that influence in Skip's brain speaks volumes as to what type of people Van Halen are and were. Skip was around them, spoke with them, and guarded them and their wives. Skip was on-duty, paying full attention to them, explaining, assessing, communicating, and moreover, Skip's full character was on display. That is what VH saw, the same man I know, the same man Chris looks up to and adores unconditionally. Van Halen was a part of Skip's world. Van Halen gave him respect, for he deserved it—and that was mutual, for it was reciprocated back to the band as well.

Listen to some music, watch over the boys, and enjoy himself—that is what Mr. Myres did that night—he was the father-figure, acting like a Boy Scout—he was prepared. Having been through numerous adventures with his family, Mr. Myres was battle tested and all set to dive right into the seen, which means he will be able to understand the words coming out of their mouths. "I was the only one in the audience that could hear the concert, the sound was so powerful—the rest of you people only heard white noise." Mr. Myres stated—"That is still the reason I have ringing in my ears." As noted earlier, bees wax allowed him to take in the cords and the riffs of Van Halen, so while me and all my buddy's and Jimmy with his friends by Michael Anthony, were yelling and screaming. Mr. M was able to enjoy the melodies for what they were, and even understanding who he was watching. Allowing him to gain a step up on all the other attendees, and this band jamming it out on stage. "I was aware of Van Halen, I knew who they were, that's all the kids talked about—that was during the days of *MTV*, unlike today, it was all music videos." He said, as he attempted his own drum solo at the dining room table. Bada Bing Bada Boom.

I grew up with Peter, Paul, and Mary, and having watched Perry Como on television, having listened to Simon and Garfunkel, Creedence Clearwater Revival, and attending a KISS concert way up in the nose-bleed section. Mr. Myres thought and assumed he was well prepared for this high-strung rock band—needless to say, he was not. There is a huge difference from row ten to way back beyond Egypt, when listening to a rock band. "The sound of Van Halen, literally pelted the crap out of me, it was so damn loud." Mr. Myres could relate to *Good Morning Vietnam,* where Bob, the caller, tells Robin Williams' character (Adrian Cronauer), "Play anything, just play it loud."

There is a difference between bingo night at the VFW hall and seeing Van Halen. There is even a bigger difference between attending church and seeing Van Halen. The mosh pit was not a term back in '84, but front row seating was. Dancing aggressively, jumping, bumping, and slamming into each other was not even perceived as something to worry about in '84, but this was Van Halen, with the number one hit, *JUMP.* We all knew it was going to be amazing. Mr. Myres and all of us were taken aback at our seat assignments. "We were not sitting in church benches that night, we were standing on these flimsy chairs, we had to stand the whole time—Who's idea was this? No dancing in the aisles that night." Mr. Myres explained as to why his dogs were barking—standing the whole duration, yelling, screaming kids and young adults all over the place. Van Halen displaying their full energy, and there we all were. Like he said, standing and enjoying the evening's entertainment. There were no complaints that night, not one peep of dishonoring the band or the facility. It wasn't until forty years later, that we all realized how crazy it was at thirteen years old, to be that close, pay only $12.50 per ticket and witness Van Halen put on an amazing show.

I sat down with Jimmy Myres and the first question I fired his way was, what does Van Halen mean to you? Instantly, without any hesitation or pondering either, the words rolled out in a flash. "Van Halen equals rock 'n' roll, in a nutshell." To describe Van Halen is hard to do for so many people—fans experience rock 'n' roll in so many different fashions it sometimes gets cloudy or disjointed when describing a band, one has seen. For Jimmy, he instantly conjured up the best description any band would want to hear, they equal "rock 'n' roll."

Who is your favorite band? Can you name them all, including the bass player? It's easy to rattle off the lead singer, or the guitar player, or even the drummer, but the bass player, well that gets a little tricky. My concert going pals can fire off those names as quickly as reciting the ABCs. Van Halen was welcomed into our homes, well before we all saw them in person. They had a beat to them, a look to them, a zealous point man, two brothers, and a bassist that was a part of the stage performance. They were "the greatest show on earth."

Jimmy and I began to talk about David Lee Roth, which went into a huge gritty smile over Jimmy's face. "David Lee Roth is a hell of a showman," Jimmy replied quickly and assertively. A showman, to put on a show—the front man of the band—the lead singer, the man on center-stage. His energy that night, directly represents the enthusiasm he carries with him all the time—smile, pizzaz, outlandish outfits and hairdo, fast talker, the ladies' man to say the least, the L.A. scene and girls, girls, and more girls. This was 1984, and he was knee deep in bikinis, palm trees, the ocean, and being the epicenter of a major rock 'n' roll band. It's fun to visualize seeing David on stage that night—flying around like a chicken with its head cut off—leftside, rightside, center stage, behind the drums, with Eddie, and singing with Michael. It didn't matter, the spotlight was following him around with pinpoint precision. Jimmy having attended numerous concerts, put it like this, "David lee Rot., Still given'em hell after all these years."

Jimmy and I kept laughing and reminiscing about David's performance that night, but what stood out to Jimmy even more, was he was able to obtain better seats, and lo and behold it was right next to the leftside, facing the stage, adjacent to Michael Anthony. "Michael Anthony, you Mother F**cker!!!" Jimmy and his buddy kept yelling. From what Jimmy shared with me, he was yelling and screaming at the top of his lungs—hook, line, and sinker—Jimmy was reeled in, he had caught the big one—

in this case, the ideal seat. "Michael was 100% invested that night. He kept throwing his pics our way, and I caught three of them—then the next day in my army jacket I found another one." Being a part of something truly amazing is one thing, to own a piece of the arena, is another—then to add four bass pics to his arsenal of merchandise, that my friends is pure bliss, to a seventeen-year-old. A Van Halen fan long before that night, and this just amplified why Jimmy is a Van Halen fan. They all put on a show that night, and Jimmy was right there in the thick of it. Interacting with Michael, as if they had known each other for years, Jimmy was a part of their band/family that evening.

Jimmy shared with me, that he had seen many drummers perform before attending the VH concert—he rattled off at least fifteen drummer's names, which cascaded into Alex Van Halen. "The drum solo, was bump, bump, bump—and fast as hell at the end." Air guitar is very common today, because everyone feels they can carry a tune or two—but an air drummer, now that takes some skill. Jimmy went into full Alex right there in the middle of the library, while conducting our interview. His performance was done without a glitch, no hesitation at all. It's one thing to play the drums, but to be toe-tapping as well, Jimmy nailed it—and I know if Alex was in the room, instantly he would have said, "All hail Jimmy!!!!!"

"Van Halen! My favorite band of all time!" A fan told me that, that fan is Todd Zimmerman. It's difficult to amass such a following as Van Halen did. To have the best lead singer, the best drummer, the best bassist, and the best guitar player (to Todd and me), all tangled up in one band—that is hard to accomplish and segue from album to album, and from song to song. Van Halen created five previous albums, *1984* being sixth, turned Todd into a fan forever, having seen them live in concert.

Todd's grandma thought Satan lived in his bedroom because of the Iron Maiden poster. She imagined Todd's head spinning, puking his guts out, levitating and speaking fluent Latin. No, Todd was far removed from that scene. We all were. We were altar boys, good Catholic young men, well at least 90% of the time we were—but hey, we were testing the waters, and the older boys were having an influence over us. Shout out to Jim Jr. Music was on a high note (yes, pun intended) and *MTV* was our outlet. Numerous hours were dedicated to just about any type of music. The only question was, will our parents say anything about hard-core heavy metal? My parents did, Todd's did, and I know Chris' did too—Mike on the other hand had a terrific gift, an older brother. "Heavy hard rock bands were blowing up in the 80s, but they were hardcore. Van Halen seemed to be one notch down from them." Todd explained to me and looking around either side, as if his parents were still present to correct him. Van Halen set the tone in the Zimmerman household, as they did in mine. They were a breakout band with *MTV*, hitting their peak and taking off in 1984. Music was being introduced to us from all directions; the radio, LPs, cassettes, and of course TV—*Solid Gold, Soul Train,* and *MTV*.

Besides *Jump*—can you name ten other Van Halen songs from the top of your head? No *Google* search, just rattle them off. If you're a raving fan it is easy, if you're just a fan it's easy. Now, what is your favorite Van Halen song? I asked Todd this question and he immediately rolled into an unbelievable response. "If someone was to ask me, what is my least favorite Van Halen song—I don't know if I can answer that, it is not about the music, it's about the band, and what I grew up with, and I have committed my life as a fan, so their all my favorites."

Ken Blanchard wrote a super book called, *Raving Fans*, which was written, to bring to fruition that customers want more. They don't want average. They don't want fair or medium—they want well-done. We want a 5-star hotel experience, on a 3-star budget. Van Halen is that 5-star, thus creating fans for life. Todd goes on to explain the in-person experience, "I remember back in '83 and '84, racing off the school bus to try and catch Van Halen on *MTV*. Hoping to catch the *Jump* video. *Jump*!!!! When that video came on *MTV*, my VCR was at the ready to record. I played it over and over, but that night seeing Van Halen in person, only having known them through the *JUMP* video was something out of this world. To see them live, to hear them live, and feel them live, it was a WOW moment. It was nothing like watching them on TV, it was a thousand times better." Todd became a fan for life, just like the old Memorex commercial slogan, "Is it live or is it Memorex?" Todd now knows the difference. Being in attendance that night and listening to Van Halen today—two different sides to a coin. Sure, it may not shatter a glass, but instantly Todd is taken back to Cincinnati Gardens. Any Van Halen song shatters Todd's chain of thought, it breaks it up instantly, transports him to row 10, and he can visualize seeing *JUMP* in person, LIVE......

"The music of my childhood, from fifth grade up through high school was Van Halen." Seven solid years of nothing but Van Halen, Mike explained. He went from only listening to them for two years, then seeing them in person, then round after round of purchasing music, then going to the concert, talking about the concert, and allowing others into his lively world of Van Halen. A band's vision is to welcome others into their space, into their lives and into their concert in harmony. Allowing fans to experience their music is powerful, and as a youngster, Van Halen reeled Mike in.

"Dad, will you tape Johnny Carson, Van Halen will be on—or Valeri Bertinelli was on. Any interview, that had everything and anything to do with Van Halen, I had to watch it." Todd laughed with excitement—but it was true, in what he said. Van Halen was the band. VH was the rock group. They were the talk of the town and the talk of the year. Todd was the right age, and he was in line with them.

Only a few things stand out that night to Todd. It was forty years ago...A lot to remember for an *AARP* card carrying member. (Just joking. No clue if Todd carries one, but he is old enough.....LOL) "David lee Roth is a showman; he was leading the crowd—his kicks and his jumps were just awesome. The gong was set ablaze by Alex. Michael pounding his bass and Eddie's magic on the guitar." That's what Todd remembers. And that is why Todd is a raving fan.

I asked Chris if he remembered the high school girl that came and stood with us at the concert—he didn't remember. I asked Todd the same question, and he could not remember it either. In speaking with Mike, I asked him if he remembered the girl who stood next to us at the concert. "Of course, I do. But I doubt she remember us," Mike said with laughter. To lay out the image, it was Mr. Myres, then me, because Mike did not want to stand next to his dad, so Mike on my right and his dad was on my left. Van Halen had just started to play and here comes this girl with the huge 80s hair, she looked at Mike and me and asked if she could stand between us. "Yes, and Yes." For the record I can't remember what she looked like, but I do remember what she smelled like—Aqua Net hairspray. With the skunk smell in the air, a girl in Mike's and my arms, Van Halen playing—Mike and I were officially introduced to sex, drugs and rock 'n' roll. Mike and I both remember our arms around her, and her arms around us. Now the concert was 100% complete, just like all the videos on *MTV*—we had a girl with us.

Van Halen has a different meaning to each of us guys. Mike's reaction, when I asked him about Van Halen, instantly took him back to grade school, and one of our fellow classmates. Mike stated, "When I think of Van Halen in grade school, I think of Terri Bolger—she loved Van Halen and knew that I did too. She had older brothers, which gave her access to rock magazines. She would bring in the Eddie, or Alex pictures, and give me the David and Michael posters that came in them—I plastered my bedroom wall with all those pics."

On *themightyvanhalen*.net
Here is the set list from the Cincinnati Gardens concert, back in 1984.
What is unbelievable, if you check that site out, there is a bootleg version
of *Unchained* uploaded of that night, forty years ago.

1. *Unchained*
2. *Hot For Teacher*
3. Alex Van Halen drum solo
4. *On Fire*
5. *Running With the Devil*
6. *Dave Talks*
7. *Little Guitars*
8. *Cathedral*
9. *House of Pain*
10. Michael Anthony bass solo
11. *Jamie's Cryin*
12. *I'll Wait*
13. *Keyboard Solo*
14. *Everybody Wants Some!!*
15. *Girl Gone Bad*
16. *1984*
17. *Jump*
18. Eddie Van Halen guitar solo
19. *Oh, Pretty Woman*
20. *Panama*
21. *You Really Got Me* **encore**
22. *Ain't Talkin' Bout Love* **encore**

Eddie's Death

Celebrities, to me, have always been an escape route from reality—from movies, to plays, to sporting events. I have hunkered down for hours and have watched the Super Bowl. I have hunkered down for hours and watched a play-off game, or even The Masters and I, as well as you, have been excited to attend a first run movie. We have all been there, waiting in line to purchase our ticket to see the big movie on the big screen. I have never met Arnold Schwarzenegger or Lou Ferrigno, two men that I looked up to as a teenager—from *Conan The Barbarian* and *The Incredible Hulk*. I have watched *E.T.* a zillion times, and recall Michelle Holifield, taking me and her brother Johnny to see the movie. I have yet to meet Drew Barrymore—but to have seen someone in person, at such a young age, at the height of their career, well that is something powerful.

It was October 6, 2020, when Eddie Van Halen was taken from us, at the age of sixty-five on up through the *Stairway to Heaven*, a song that hit home the day I heard of his passing. I have never been one to worship celebrities. I have never followed their guidance, bought into their cosmetics, power drinks, or even bought a home gym, and yet here I was at forty-nine, getting wind that the great legendary guitar HERO had passed away. My heart sank that day, I was saddened to hear of him passing through the pearly gates.

To grow up with someone, and to idolize someone is a piece of history that we all carry with us in one fashion or another. We all know who we wanted to be like, look like, and in Eddie's case, sound like. People would mimic him, his hairdo, the clothes, the sounds, the tapping of the strings, the smile on his face, and even wanting the girl that he had, Valerie. He had all the glamour, and the handsome grit to his personality. He was lively, energetic, and charismatic. Men wanted to be him, and girls wanted to be with him. He was a sought-after man, for his fingers were a work of magic. They were as fast as anyone's out there, for he was the line leader to me.

The instant I heard of Eddie's passing, I was taken back to March 9, 1984—having watched him run the stage, riff on his Frankenstein, sing in melody with his friends, and give the best concert a young man could see with these innocent eyes. Sad, yet happy at the same time when I got wind of his death, because it takes me back to that wonderful day, a day that Eddie and Van Halen gave my buddies and me. It is a moment that I can never relive, yet in writing this book and reveling in those moments and expressing friendship, Eddie Van Halen gave me the best moment of my life at such a young age. I was there to bear witness to his magic, his gift from God. Eddie went out and rocked the stage and gave all of us one hell of a concert.

Death is inevitable, it will happen to us all. There is an old saying that goes, you only live once, yet that same slogan was contradicted by many authors, and it reads like this, "You live every day, you die only once." Eddie lived life to the fullest, he gave thousands of teenagers his gift of living so many times over. He produced so many albums, so many songs, so many live concerts, that the day Eddie passed a little bit of me passed away too, as well as millions of fans worldwide—Eddie was in us all growing up in the 80s—watching *MTV*, flipping through *Guitar* magazine, *Hit Parade* and *Spin*.

Sadness will come over me again for certain celebrities that I grew up with. I know it, I will feel it, but I will appreciate their gift to me. I will honor their legacy and I will pass down to my kids the entertainment value they gave to me. My love of music is because of Eddie and Van Halen. The $12.50 ticket was the greatest purchase of the musical side of my life.

Moments like these, come across our table but only a handful of times. My parents allowing me to see Eddie was really the ultimate gift my parents ever gave me—they unleashed a boy and created a man that night. As crazy as it sounds, by seeing Eddie in person, I had a forever connection with him and his guitar. It's a bond that will never be broken, never be forgotten, and a story that will live on forever. Eddie Van Halen, God rest your soul. But, while you are up in Heaven, I hope you introduce yourself to my mom, my dad, Chris' mom, and Mike's mom—for I know they would love to meet you.

To all the parents out there who allowed their kids to attend a rock concert, I say job well done—scared, frightened, worried, all those adjectives are understandable, but to be able to say "Yes", when it was so easy to say "No"—well that is the gift you gave your children, the gift of rock 'n' roll. Now that I am in my fifties, as well as folks out there that saw Van Halen live all those years ago, you are now parents and grandparents—so when your child or grandchild says, "Can I go to a concert?" Think of what Eddie and Van Halen gave to you and say YES—allow the next generation to experience their band, their melody, what rocks their world.

A friend of mine shared a story about the '85 Chicago Bears. He was watching the Super Bowl with all of his friends, and when the Bears won, everyone was screaming and running around the house. He ran up to his dad in the other room and said, "We won! We Won!" —his dad then said, "Does that mean we don't go to work tomorrow? Should I quit my job and party? Life goes on, it's just football and a Super Bowl win doesn't pay our bills." It is true, worshipping celebrities, running off to buy all their novelty items is not exactly what our parents wanted us to do with our money as youngsters, or even adults—but celebrities, bands, groups, singers, they all give us, even just a few hours of an escape, a getaway, a time to unravel.

I read a book about taking vacation, in that if you need a getaway from reality, then you should change your reality. You should get a different job or drive a different way to work—I whole heartedly disagree with my friend's dad and the author of that book. Vacation is a time to experience new things, see new countries, new beaches, mountain climb, jet ski, snow ski—whatever you need to recharge those batteries. Watching the Super Bowl is the same thing. It is the camaraderie of buddies watching a game, laughing, yelling, and going crazy that brings positive moments to oneself.

Eddie's death, as tragic as it was, is a gift to us all. So many people have talents, and there are so many gifted people out there. Quick, what was the name of that author who gave up????? What was the name of that baseball player who quit????? What was the name of that band who folded?? Exactly, no one remembers their names. They are gone, they quit at an early age. Eddie and Van Halen never gave up, they kept going and going and going—they were the real-life Energizer bunny. Eddie's guitars on display at the Rock 'n' Roll Hall of Fame prove that we should follow our dreams, pursue them in whatever fashion we can. Eddie got his 10,000 hours in to become an expert. I got to see him at the height of his career, that is the gift I received from him.

Sadness will be experienced by all of us. It is a part of growing up, and it is a fact of life. It is only a matter of time until we can't do certain things any longer. We are limited due to our physical capabilities, so at a young age, just like my buddies and I did—go out and see that band. See that concert and forever be bonded with them.

"I was working from home that day, and I saw the headline pop-up, that Eddie had passed away." Chris said with an edge of sadness in his tone, "There is no way." Chris went onto share what his first thoughts were, "That is the end of the guitar generation. He was the greatest, what he could do with the guitar, it was like it was talking to us. You could hear words when he was playing the guitar. It always amazed me the way his fingers worked; it was so effortless. My thoughts were, we lost one of the greatest, if not the greatest guitar player. Then after that all the memories of all the times, I had seen him in concert., sunk in. I just sat back in my chair and thanked him for giving me the best memories, not only him but the band as well."

Skip Berger reflected on his death, "Eddie Van Halen, I only knew him briefly, to me he was a nice guy. Down to earth. We talked before the concert; I really liked the guy from the time I met him. I can really tell a lot about people very quickly, straight shooting guy—I liked him." Straight out of Skip's mouth, not preplanned at all. Factual statement. "I was sad. I felt for his family and for everyone who knew him. I felt bad, and felt it was a passing of the experience that Chris and I had. I thought about that. I flashed back to that, and I thought WOW!! I could see him standing there in the hallway and talking to him—seeing how his hair was, how he was dressed. I was touched. People think that when well-known people die that they had a connection with them, but I did. It was very small, but I had connection," Skip said.

"For me the day Eddie passed was a block removed from me, a piece of my past that is gone—I was in disbelief," Jimmy shared. He went on, "He is not replaceable. He is one of a kind. He paved the way for so many guitar players." The words of a true rock fan.

"The show must go on. "How many times have we heard that? Millions and millions—but that is a true testament to Eddie and all of Van Halen. "Hey, what's this lying around Shi*T? Over! Over! Did you say over? Nothing is over, until we decide it is. Was it over when the Germans bombed Pearl Harbor? Hell No! And it ain't over now. Because when the going gets tough………….the tough get going. Who's with me? Let's Go!!!!!!!" Bluto's speech in *Animal House*. Jimmy's comment on the next generation of guitar players, exemplifies that the torch has been passed, and the fire is not out—the flame is kept alive. "It was a real surprise, I know he (Eddie) had more to give, and it's just not there now. Although his son does a hell of job. I was skeptical at first, but Wolfgang is unbelievable too." That's the message to all, Wolfgang under his own guidance will continue the Eddie Van Halen legacy, but it will be under his skills, his mindset, and his passion. Sure, Wolfgang will play some VH tunes, tap some fingers like his dad—Wolfgang must be Wolfgang, that is the true spirit that Jimmy saw in him—that we see Eddie. No one can replace anyone, at a high level of competition. Its why legends are created, and why Hall-of-Famers and statues are created. So that we never forget.

If two people get the walk sign to cross the street and one gets hit by a car, that equates to being at the right place at the wrong time. If the other crosses the street without injury, then that is being at right place at the right time. Now, two people are jaywalking, one is hit and the other makes it across—wrong place at the wrong time, the other person, wrong place at the right time. That was 1984, we all were in the right year, at the right time, to listen to Van Halen. Others were listening to kinder, gentler music. Who is the best guitar player? That conversation comes up all the time. Everyone will argue about it. Jimmy Page. Eric Clapton. Jimi Hendrix. "To this day, I still say it is Eddie. That solo was so amazing." Todd shared his expert analysis. It is true. My parents grew up with Eric and Jimmy, as well as Jimi—flower children, not really. Although I do share a fictious story often that my parents met at Woodstock—Dad was "high" at the top of the hill, and Mom was naked at the bottom, and it was pouring down rain. Dad slid down the hill and took Mom's feet out and two hours later I was conceived, with the National Anthem playing in the background. My parents thought John Denver was a great guitar player, they loved George Harrison, and enjoyed Roy Orbison and many others. That's who they grew up with, and that's who they knew when raising two boys, working full-time, paying the mortgage and coaching baseball. Eddie Van Halen, who was he? All they knew was he was a guitar player, and in the video *JUMP*. Wrong place at the right time. That's just how it will always be. What we grew up with was Eddie and Van Halen, right age, and the right year.

"Eddie's death was a loss for the music community," Mike said recalling that day. "It's one thing to see a celebrity on TV, and to see a celebrity live in person. So, Eddie's death had more meaning to me, for I had seen him perform live." Mike justifies the reason fans take it on the chin at the passing of a celebrity. Eddie was a part of our past, and we held a slight bond or connection with him, and now he is gone forever. The good news is that Mike got to experience Eddie's talent first-hand. Mike not only can still listen to his solos, but Mike can also say I have seen him in person, that is the gift Eddie gave us all.

"When celebrities die, you always say awe......or that's sad. That day upon hearing Eddie passed away, well, that just sucked. Eddie was a good dude, it hit me hard—I was upset about that," Todd's not one to weep or feel sad—he is a sailor for God's sake, tough as nails. But a passing is a passing, and when that person is a part of your life, having never met them, but being influenced by them, it hits home. My dad always told me that there are three types of funerals—sad, didn't see that coming, and celebrated. He defined them by the age in which the person passed, One, under the age of thirty, is sad. Two, between thirty and sixty, didn't see that coming. Three, sixty and older, we need to celebrate their life. Eddie was sixty-five years-old when he passed. As sad as it is, he gave so much, shared so much, and influenced so many that from a selfish standpoint, I wish he was still alive. The music industry misses him. I miss him. We all miss him. It was a celebrated life, and the magic that he gave us, will last an eternity. People will tell stories about him, mimic his playing abilities, name babies after him, name guitars and amplifiers after him. His legacy is as solid as it can be.

There is a picture that circulates all around social media of Eddie Van Halen holding an index card, with the words, I WILL ALWAYS BE WITH

YOU.... JUST PRESS PLAY. I have no idea if that picture is even real or was photoshopped, but it is moving. The words in that image speak to us all. No matter where we are, or what we are doing, just hit play and we are instantly mesmerized by the steadfast fingers and catching smile of Eddie.

In 1985, Chris Berger was given an actual photo of Eddie Van Halen from his mom and dad. The picture was of Eddie wearing this same shirt—with a huge smile on his face. All who appreciate Eddie, can connect with his smile. He always happy, and thrilled to be doing what he was doing, playing guitar, and loving the music industry. Some years ago, Chris decided that he needed the same shirt—so like all true fans, he look online for what he wanted, and purchase it.

Musical Monday Mornings

Jump, Running with the Devil, Little Guitars, D.O.A, Tora! Tora! You Really Got Me. Those songs are what send chills down my spine the minute I hear them, any song Van Halen has sung instantly takes me back to 1984. Music is so powerful to me today at fifty-three years old, the guy who was never into music growing up. Today I drown in the melodies flowing through the speakers of my car. Instantly it takes me to a time and a place, music has that way about it. What is your favorite song and why? Prom, wedding night, first kiss, first concert, road trip with the guys, road trip with your family? *SpongeBob* even has that grabbing action with me, the minute I hear the melody to *SpongeBob*, it takes me back to when my daughter and I would watch that crazy sponge talk and sing with that goofy star, Patrick. It was always a fun thirty minutes for her and me, just the two us watching TV, laughing, smiling and giggling. I can still hear Maggie's laugh through the words *SpongeBob*.

I have been to many concerts, not as many as Jimmy, Chris or Todd— but my fair share, and I have had the privilege to have two parents that loved music. That trait was passed down to me. Certain songs move me from excitement, to sadness, to reflection, to anger. The special ones take me back to a certain place and time. They strike my nervous system and enable me to instantly recall a moment from my past.

Musical Monday Mornings is that program that always does that for me. Musical Mondays is a program down at the local library that my wife Gina puts on the third Monday of each month. She chooses a musical, and takes center stage, engrossing all in attendance with the ins and outs of the musical. The past cast and/or current cast, the history behind the musical, where it originated, who sang the songs—you get the point.

The minute the clock strikes 11 a.m., Gina turns into the forgotten cast member, or the documentary expert behind the scenes. and share with us all the magic that made that musical so famous. *Fiddler on the Roof* was one of the first musicals that she presented. The minute she explained the history I was taken back to a moment, a precious moment, when she and I went to see a live performance of it. It instantly hit my heart and my eyes began to swell up with tears. I did my best not to cry, there is no crying in baseball, but hey this is fun—so I acted like I sneezed, when in reality I was wiping away my tears. That night with her, was just so much fun. I knew all the songs leading up to curtain call, because my parents would play that LP in the house when I was a kid. Two fond memories because of *Fiddler on the Roof*. It was so powerful. I could feel goosebumps come over me, the hair stood up, my heart was racing, because I loved that day with her. Then, Gina put up on a screen the lyrics to the famous songs from the musical, and we all sang along with the piano player, Char, seated in the corner. In harmony we all sang *Tradition*,

Match Maker, If I were A Rich Man, and I was taken back to my parents' house in the living room where my mom and dad would sing those songs. They loved the play and musical, and I remember looking at them as if they were weird, crazy or had gone mad. How wrong I was then, and I am so glad those positive thoughts of my parents come over me today.

The next musical that Gina did was *Mamma Mia!* ABBA, now that was a band that was always on the record player back in grade school. Once again, the memory bank door was opened wide, and goosebumps came over me, and tears began to well up—in the summer of 2022 my mom passed away from ALS, horrible disease, yet I can't remember that grotesque disease, because I cherish all the positive moments I had with my mom. When she would play her ABBA, she would drag my brother and me into the living room, and she would teach us both how to dance. I would say no way, I am sure, but today I remember her dancing, laughing, and just having the time of her life because I was dancing with her, Dad was dancing, and my brother was too. She used to say, "You both are getting older, dances are coming up in high school, and you must learn to dance. You don't want to be known as the guys standing on the sidelines holding the wall up." She was aggressive, but compassionate, and knew we had to learn. So, with *Super Trooper, SOS, Take a Chance on Me* playing through the speakers, I learned to dance. And guess what? In high school I had the moves on the floor—I knew a step or two....

The next Musical Monday Mornings was Christmas tunes, and there was Gina taking center stage, with a packed house, twenty or so adults all listening to her presentation. She told us the history of a few Christmas tunes, where and when they were created, and shared some holiday trivia. She pointed to the piano, and without a hitch, *White Christmas* was being sung by everyone in unison. The piano was in tune and once again, tears began streaming down my eyes. Christmas, I have loved it for so long, but to hear us all singing, took me back to when we, as a family, would drive to downtown Cincinnati. We would grab a nice dinner, do a little window shopping, look at all of the Christmas decorations, and pick out a Christmas ornament. From the minute we got in the car to start our Christmas tradition, Dad had the station tuned to Christmas music. Then after seeing the awesome displays downtown, on the back way home we would drive around the neighborhoods looking at all the Christmas lights. One song, after another took me back to those days. I can tell you where we ate, what ornament I got, and I will never forget the one blue light, that we only saw once. One house had a plastic candle in the top right window, with a blue lightbulb. To this day, I still remember the one blue light, back then in the 70s folks appreciated the cops, looked up to them, and respected them. Maybe that was foreshadowing to always remember the men and women in BLUE.

Right as the book was about to go to the editor, Gina pulled out on more Musical Monday Mornings—this time she did Motown. Hit after hit was on my sheet of songs we were about to sing. The very first song was *Dancing in the Street*, which in 1964, Martha and the Vandellas sang, hitting No. 2 on the *Billboard Hot 100* chart. Here we were in 2023, singing this song, and the first thing that came to my mind was Van Halen. Unbeknownst to Gina, Van Halen did a cover of this song on their *Diver Down* album, which was released in 1982. Van Halen took that song to No. 38 on the *Billboard Hot 100* chart.

Every Christmas through high school, my parents took us downtown, and this was when piano bars were popular. I can still picture the piano player in the corner headlining and lit candles as the center piece. Joe's Bar was our hot spot. Dad would take clients from out of town there. Mom and Dad would head there on weekends, maybe as a date, a quick bite before a show, or to meet up with other couples. One night as we sat down, over in the corner was Mr. Brophy moving his fingers and singing a tune. Mr. Brophy was our grade school music teacher, and he was the night's entertainment. How cool was that. We are in this adult atmosphere and here our music teacher playing the piano. I can still see the tables jam full with customers tapping their feet, singing along, and chatting up a storm. Smoke filled room, high balls all over the place, beer mugs full, it was glamorous—it was as if we were in Casablanca. I felt so adult with my kiddy cocktail in my hand. Mr. Brophy even had recorded an album, which he was selling that night. Seeing someone that we knew personally singing and performing is very uplifting. He knew our names, and that was powerful as a young man. Someone we looked up to came over to our table, shook our hands, and extended a thank you for coming. Of course, we expressed how wonderful he was too. He was a celebrity to me, he was a musical icon, and my family and I knew him.

Music has a way of triggering memories that I have forgotten about, and always reel me in the moment I hear a certain tune. The minute I hear *Jet Airliner* by Steve Miller Band, I am taken back to Joe Lisi's campsite down on the Ohio River. I can still recall all that took place there in high school, at his grandpa's campsite. A lot of beer was consumed, songs were blasted, card games were played, and we all partied. It was a fun spot, and it seemed as if Steve Miller Band was on all the time, a constant loop. The Doors' one song, *Peace Frog*—that tune from the *Morrison Hotel* album instantly makes me think of my dear friend Tommy Pieples, his family and he are the best. The minute I hear that song it takes me back to every single memory that Tommy and I had together...

from basketball, to baseball, to summer festivals and of course all of our grade school shenanigans. The whole Pieples family: Gary, Gregg, Jill, Lori and of course his mom and dad, Tom and Charlene instantly flash memories of my past that I cherish. Bob Seger's *Night Moves*, when I hear that one song, it instantly takes me back to when I learned how to drywall at Chuck Heckler's house. His wife and he were redoing their ceiling at their house, and Bob's CD was on in the background, on a constant loop. We were drinking beer while putting it up, and we were laughing and having fun remodeling his sunroom. The Firm's *Radioactive*, that song reminds me of my brother, since he was a massive Led Zeppelin fan. He had never seen Jimmy Paige because Led Zeppelin broke up when he was only eight. Now here he was, able to hear Jimmy Paige with a new band, The Honeydrippers. Their song *Sea of Love,* now when I hear that song, I instantly think of the video on *MTV.* I just laugh and laugh, because there is a very thin, mustachioed guy playing the steelpan in the background, wearing a red speedo. Now without saying names, my family would just laugh hysterically at that video, for we swore that was our next-door neighbor in that video. We would yell from the other room to Mom and Dad, "Our neighbor is on again. Get in here." They would say, "Yep, that must be him." It wasn't, but damn dead on. Another song that instantly grabs me is, *Welcome to The Jungle* by Guns N' Roses. It makes me think of the Cincinnati Bengals, and the years I had season tickets. Then there is one tune, which was a big 80s hit by the Beach Boys, that makes me think of high school, and the year some of my classmates performed *Kokomo* on stage, in front of the whole school. Chris Kowalak, Stacy Smith, and John Mulvey come to mind when I hear that yacht tune—it was just as fun in '89, as it is today, in 2024.

There is something gripping about words that pull us into our subconscious, like "I'll be back!" "Feel lucky punk?" "E.T. phone home." Those are just a few, I am sure you can rattle others off quickly. What is that song, or songs, or bands that gets your groove on? Which tune gets your blood pumping and gets you excited? Can you correlate that rhythm to a moment in time that floods you with memories? It's the same way with a scent, like aftershave or freshly cut grass, but music does it to me like no other method. The theme to *Cheers* makes me recall beanbag chair. The *Star Wars* theme makes me think of the game, bury the *Star Wars* figures, that my brother and I invented and played. The rules were simple, we would kill them, then go off to the woods and bury them. Musical Monday Mornings, is without a doubt a positive journey down memory lane. I feel the nostalgia and I can see that other participants do too. With their feet tapping, their voices blaring—it works for them, as it does for me.

Panama, Eruption, Runnin' with the Devil, Mean Street, Jump, and of course *Unchained,* each song makes me sing loud and far for all to hear. I love it, for my life was blessed that night 40 years ago, because I was allowed to attend a grown-up event with all of my grade school friends. We saw the hottest band in America and the world in 1984. It was rocking.

"My parents didn't go to a lot of concerts, they were busy raising eight kids, but I do remember them always playing music," Jimmy reflects. "My mom gave me the album, *At Filmore East,* by The Allman Brothers Band. Mom listened to Barry Manilow, Neil Diamond, and a slew of others. They definitely were a musical influence." Mike agreed as he rattled off the same musician, without knowing Jimmy had already let the cat out of the bag, "Mom listened to Neil Diamond." Two boys, vividly remembering their mom (Barb) playing LPs in the house and can even name the same artist.

"He may have taken a few lessons."—that is what folks would say if they heard Mike play the piano today. He shared with me, "I played piano for twelve years; I am not too good." Not that good, compared to someone who can't even play, is considered a master. To be able to read music is a gift, and to play is a talent. Mike therefore is talented. Is he going to play at Music Hall? Probably not. But the artistic side of Mike is there, the musical side of Mike is there, and just like his mom, the gift of music was passed down from one generation to the next. That is the power of positive influence. Mike has the gift to pound on the piano, play tunes, gather friends and family around and play a few notes. Mike is musically inclined.

"Mom was very into music, her bother Tom was into music, and was in a band in high school and college, he was the drummer." Jimmy stated, then immediately went on about another influence in the family. "Uncle Tom was a great musician, and Mom could play the piano. It is still in the living room today." When I went over to interview Mr. Myres, the piano was right there in the living room. It is still in working fashion, still a talking piece, and still an item that can bring the family into another room. Imagine all the songs that family could sing in harmony—they were the real-life *Partridge Family.* Eight kids all singing Christmas songs, and of course Mike could play as well. With that, Mike could take the lead— music was flowing like a stream at the Myres' compound.

Jimmy Myres put into context Mike's ability to play the piano. "Mike is a great piano player, ask him to play Charlie Brown—FEARLESS.....I was always amazed how he could play by ear. Some people just have the gift, and Mike has it." I am sure as teenagers growing up in the Myres house, Jimmy held back his words to his brother. The older we get, the more appreciative we are of talent—here he is giving Mike a pat on the back. In high school it was more of a punch on the shoulder. Big brother saying this of Mike will hit home, a statement of true musical feelings for his abilities.

sometimes it only takes one song to bring back a thousand memories

-Unknown

Leadership

In looking back at the Van Halen concert, it took a mountain of leadership to forge my way to where I am today—leadership is and always will be a linchpin in my life, I have carried that word with me for years and years, for all of us in one fashion or another are in leadership. A single woman to her cat is a leader, a father of three with a wife and two dogs is a leader...to understand what a leader is, is to look into the eyes of another and ask yourself does this person make me want to do better? In developing people from all walks of life—in the book *Leadership Excellence: The Seven Sides of Leadership for the 21st Century* by Pat Williams he created 7 columns for holding up the word leadership and these are the seven from the book. Look them over. Are they in your life? Did people help you with those words? Is your community using them? Your fire station, government, ball team, and for the purpose of this book did your friends' parents lead you in one fashion or another????— sometimes it takes years to see that it is prevalent. But someone, somewhere instilled values in you. Pat created this book for the 21st century, but back in '84 Mr. Myres and Mr. Berger were displaying these key pillars to all us kids. A little foreshadowing, I would say.

1. Vision
2. Communication
3. People Skills
4. Character
5. Competence
6. Boldness
7. Servant Heart

VISION

To see beyond the moment, is how I would describe vision. That night in 1984, it took vision to see through the dry ice, the fog and all the if, and, or buts going into that evening. But trust was the vision I saw in my parents. They allowed me to attend an adult evening, at thirteen. Their vision for me was what was instore next, what was Jimmy going to do next? Their vison of me was a good kid, with a side of a little polishing to fine tune him, is still requested by the higher-ups.

COMMUNICATION

Mr. Myres, "The Chaperone," telling my parents the kids were in good hands, I will protect them with my brawn, that is communication...Knowing Mr. Myres was going to see this event through from start to finish. Mr. Berger, the Cop—expressing to all the parents that he would be there, he would be in uniform, and he would protect us kids, well that volleyed back and forth to all the parents is a skill set of communicating well, be candid and straight forward.

PEOPLE SKILLS

Mr. Berger and Mr. Myres were always in my life, I was always at Mike's, playing basketball at IHM with him and seeing Mr. Myres, and playing summer baseball with Chris, therefore Mr. Berger was always there—but these two gentlemen, had skills, they had people skills. Mr. Myres still to this day has the best laugh, he is very inquisitive and always looking to chat it up with me and all of Mike's friends, he knows how to speak to others, reassure folks. Mr. Berger being a cop, understood how to defuse a situation, how to speak in a calm voice, yet still could bark when needed too—they both were used to speaking, talking, addressing others in a positive manner.

CHARACTER

Mr. Myer and Mr. Berger both had moral qualities about them that shined through and through—being a soccer coach, well that title screams leader and Mr. Berger being a police officer, that too screams morals and values that us kids looked up to.

COMPETENCE

All the parents allowing their children to be in Mr. Myres hands, knew that he had the ability to do anything successfully, he was a pharmacist, and that is tedious, mind focusing work. Mr. Berger being an officer, well he too understood too that his very presence was a sign that he was efficient.

BOLDNESS

The confidence level of Mr. Myres and Mr. Berger were a step higher than the rest. Mr. Myres with eight kids wasn't going to hold order with us, and Mr. Berger being the cop was used to holding the line—both men knew when to be stern and were not afraid for that side to be shown when order was called for.

SERVANT HEART

The ability to serve others was the key to Mr. Berger and Mr. Myres, one was a cop—out in the community helping others, the other was a pharmacist working at one of the big hospitals in the city. Both men, understood. They both had the right motivation, fathers, spouse, coaches, demanding job for others. They were the ultimate team players—

I have been an avid reader of Pat Williams (author of over 120 books) for nearly 15 years, he is an expert on leadership to say the least—when we are young, we never really grasp the concept of leadership...It's a big word, hard to define and hard to comprehend...Yet at fifty-three, Mr. Myres and Mr. Berger both extended their skills to me at such a young age—they were who I first grasped the word authority from, respect, the "Yes sir" mentality. Yes, they were my buddy's dads, but they were leading me and planting a seed for me to grow later—they in essence were developing me into the next leader. Through trust, through guidance and through the way they lead their lives—Mr. Berger and Mr. Myres, having not seen them much after high school, instilled in me what it means to be involved, to be a part of the community for so many reasons.

Taking my daughter to her first concert, well I was Mr. Myres, I drove her there, I talked to her and explained what was going on—even told her to remember where we parked. The other half of the concert, I was Mr. Berger, I was the protector, I was the one watching her back, yet still allowing her to enjoy the concert. Those leadership skills were because of Mr. Myres and Mr. Berger that night back in '84, it sounds like a broken record, but if one of those two men were missing that night, well this book would have never happened—that night never would have happened, and this positive memory would have never had taken place.

Leadership is spoken about so heavily today, yet back in the 70s and 80s it was alive and flourishing, we just didn't understand what the word meant—so many moving parts go into leadership, so many verbs to describe it, yet leadership is the key to any thriving person. We all have it; we all carry it inside us. It's just whether we throw the switch to use it. The VH concert welcomed me into the word trust, for nothing went wrong that night at all. No bad behavior whatsoever by any of us guys. We were under the protection of two wonderful men that night—I felt protected and secured, yet they still allowed us to have fun and "JUMP"

Having interviewed Mr. Myres and Mr. Berger, having spoken to them at each of their homes, I know they both were leaders beyond their years back in 1984—I was not aware that Mr. Myres was in the coast guard. I thank him and salute him for his service. HM1 (E-6) 1966-1970. The little hidden characteristics, that us kids were not aware of, which exemplifies his understanding of maneuvering a team.

According to *Coastguard Watch Officer*—these qualities are what you need.

1. Relevant maritime skills
2. Knowledge of meteorology
3. Good verbal and written communication skills
4. Interpersonal skills
5. Good organizational skills
6. High levels of concentration
7. Strong teamwork and project management skills
8. Supervisory and people management skills
9. A strong sense of responsivity
10. IT and Keyboard skills
11. Numeracy and literacy skills to required standards
12. Customer service skills
13. A good standard of eyesight and hearing

According to *Police Chief Magazine*—these are qualities that are needed.

1. Active listening
2. Education

When we are young, we see things through a kaleidoscope, ever evolving and changing. We are seeing things only in color, for what they appear to be, not really understanding that there is black and white in our life, or even grey for that matter—we see things as happy, joyous, and everlasting, not realizing that may have been one moment in time, that other parents showed us the way, because our parents allowed them to add water to our lives. Van Halen, the concert, was I believe a turning point in my young life—how cool was it to see Chris' dad in uniform that night, protecting us. From what, I have no idea. To witness Mr. Myres driving the van full of kids, his skills at driving a stick shift on the column, his laughter, his playfulness, yet protecting us kids. From what, I have no idea. Giving up his time, to be present in our lives.... That is leadership.

Row ten, "Unchained"—is what I became because of those men, I literally was living in utopia that night, it was a nirvana type feeling—I knew I was in good hands, All-state was present, but it was not Jake that was there, it was Jim and Skip.

My dad's generation, the Vietnam generation, is what allowed me to venture off and see Van Halen—drugs, sex, marijuana, I mean that stuff they were all used to, contraband, yet turn a blind eye, its harmless, it's what the young movement is about—go out and achieve something at young age, grow wings and fly—the nest will always be here if you need us, but fly and fly, go see the world, don't sit here and say I wish I would a, or could a—get off your butt and make something for yourself—

That's what Van Halen did to me, and to my buddies—we were a pack, and we are forever in the net of Van Halen, that is the leadership skills that Eddie, David, Michael, and Alex saw in themselves, and that is what they instilled in me, through some excellent coaching. But the band put a true north in our skies that night, leadership beyond what my daily routine was. I got to see skills through other people's eyes, VH and the two dads, in retrospect. Jim and Skip are a part of the band in my eyes, they are the stagehands, the ones assembling our youthful lives. I know

Jim and Skip are true leaders in their kids yes, but Todd and I fall under that umbrella as well—and both men welcomed all of us into their world.

The Van Halen story—I asked Chris how many times he had shared the Van Halen concert with his wife, "Countless times." Chris says with a huge laugh and a big smile. "We talk about it all the time, When I share the story with others—my wife at my side, she will roll her eyes and listen to it. "There is always a little bit of pieces to add, and she will say I never heard that piece before—She knows how big of a life moment this is for me." Chris stated as he pointed to a Van Halen picture on his wall, and with a smile from a proud husband. "Hold on, one more thing to add." Chris went on to say that he took his wife Molly to her first Van Halen concert. The "Balance Tour" April 19th, 1995, at Rupp Arena in Lexington, Kentucky…" Now she could understand the *1984* story better." Chris laughing again.

The Van Halen story, Chris' daughter will have friends over to the house, or a boyfriend and the story will come up. "I am fortunate to have great relationships with my daughter's friends and boyfriends. And yes, the story comes up. It's when they start talking about music, then I will share my story, and I will take them to the basement. And then I am off to the races." Chris revealed as a proud father, and rock 'n' roller. Chris said, "STOP, one more tid bit to add." "With talking to Sophie's friends, the connection that instantly gives me "Street Cred" with her friends, is when I tell them I saw *NWA* in concert. My dad is going to absolutely kill me when he reads this, because he had no idea I went to the concert. The movie *Straight Outta Compton* has a scene detailing that night in Cincinnati, and I witnessed it firsthand. *NWA* were inducted into the Rock 'n' roll HOF in 2016, and I saw them." One cool dad…….

When you think back to all the boys who were there, their dads all had been a part of a group, a team, a unit, and a squadron—Chris (cop), Mike (Coast Guard), Todd (Coast Guard) and my dad (college baseball). All these dads, have traveled, visited, and experienced events at a very young age—they in in turn were passing those values down to us—

Family, that is what was important to Skip—he went on to share with me that with all his court time was able to build up, he had all this court time, that he had saved up—he had a plethora of time—vacation time, PTO time to allow him to coach, and take his wife and kids on excursions—you could feel the pride that he had in telling me this—all that extra work built up a sheet of extra hours that he could use at his leisure, coaching the kids was a top priority—he sacrificed his free time to give back to his kids through leadership—that is powerful, to hear a person share this is. It's what makes Mr. Berger unbelievable, he could have used his time for selfish reasons—instead he used it to be with his kids and coach and lead—

Leadership comes in one fashion or another—firsthand, Skip went on to describe a captivating moment with his kids. "I took the kids on a ride down to the district headquarters, and I locked my kids up in the cell, just to give them an idea of what it felt like—and there were other inmates in the other cells."—teaching them both the value of freedom and following our moral obligations was what Skip was instilling in his kids. "I would talk to my kids about the real world with being in the police force, but I do give credit to my wife, Jan—She was the best at everything." Skip shared with me. After reading this part, Chris added a final touch to sum it up. "We go into an open cell, dad asked Scott and I to sit down on the steel bed, coming out of the wall. The second we got to it, the door slammed, and instant fear overcame us. I saw my dad looking in from a 6"x 6" window and then he was gone. It felt like we were in there forever, but it was only like two minutes."

"I'll keep an eye on you, but not a close eye." Jimmy shared of his dad, Mr. Myres. That exemplifies what Mr. Myres was all about to me and all us kids—He did not have us on leashes; He did not have on choke-collars like we were pets—Mr. Myres gave us free reign. Yet being the all-seeing eye at the same time—I'll attest all parents have eyes on the back of their heads, that night I even believe Mr. Myres head was on a swivel yet, enjoying the concert—and being a beacon of protection in case the waters became too rough.

Responsibility for your own children is a handful, now take on the challenge of being responsible for other parents' kids—that my friends is a challenge—But, in getting to know Mr. Myres through sitting down with him, it was not a big deal. It was a routine day, coaching, working at a fast passed hospital, having eight children, Mr. Myres was born to lead, it's still in his blood—he even today loads up the car and takes kids, grandkids down to see FC Cincinnati play soccer—it's who he is...The more the merrier. "I would be a nervous wreck to take my kids to a concert, then add someone else's kids to that mix." Jimmy on his dad's willingness to take on more responsibility—Mr. Myres knows how to rustle up the cattle, been doing it for years. This was not his first rodeo—which is why all the kids' parents knew we were in excellent hands.

"Trustworthy"—that's how I saw Mr. Myres.... been there done that, piece of cake—because I had experienced that before with my kids, I'd be happy to take your kids. "My dad took me and my buddies to the WEBN fireworks forty-five years ago, down on the Ohio River. Tons of alcohol flowing, we were sitting on the wall, down by a bunch of bikers, girls raising their tops—my eyes were looking that way, and my dad gave me a light slap on the back of the head and said, "Look over here." We never moved, he just said, "Keep your eyes forward." Mr. Myres could have put in effect his emergency action plan and rounded up the troops and headed home—but Mr. Myres knew this was how it was. This is how large events flowed, and he took it upon himself to make a timely decision, which was—we are staying put, we will enjoy the fireworks and the kids will have a blast. That's the message that Mr. Myres developed in Jimmy and Mike and the whole family—you can't run away from everything, good and bad things will happen, but it is how we react to the moment, is how the fireworks took place. Deal with it, don't make a big deal of it—so you saw a few boobs, things could be worst. It could be raining…. Look at the brighter side of life, and it makes for a great story.

The day after the concert, I asked Jimmy what was the breakfast table like on that Saturday? He responded quick, "My dad was probably at work or on the soccer field." To have a son describe his dad that way in a flash, Jimmy understood his dad was 100% committed to his family. Having sacrificed his time the night before, yet that Saturday morning Mr. Myres knew his responsibilities, and Jimmy knew in his heart forty years later that his dad was fully invested in this family; sons, daughters, his wife, and their dog Fred.

Leadership is a highly used word today—book after book is written on the topic, and for good reason. We need more skills than ever before. Life is fast paced, it is quick, and we need to be quick on how we react to the circumstances—but as a dad today, as Mike, Chris, Todd, and I are—What would Mr. Myres do? What would Mr. Berger do? How would they play their cards? I know how, communicate with others. Lead by example…. Show your children the way, allow them to take that giant step… Don't hold them back, be positive, give guidance, be a great coach, and be a little authoritative when need be—but allow those kids to experience life, as we have and that is what Todd did. "When TJ and Cameron were sixteen and fourteen, Weezer was playing in downtown Cincinnati, at the Horseshoe Casino—I took them, dropped them off and then picked them up when it was over—I was okay with that." Todd shared with me, about his kids attending a concert with no supervision, it was them on their own—Todd was not in attendance as he clearly shared, but through Todd's routine with his children, Todd knew they would act with caution, be smart, be aware of their surroundings, and most importantly knew they would have fun—that is the key antidote for life, having fun—Todd created future leaders, for Todd knows a thing or two about concerts…I would say Todd is a Master Concert Attender—and he knows what skills to possess to achieve a worry free, fun and entertaining event.

"By allowing my kids to venture off and see this concert, I knew they would see, hear, and experience wild stuff for the first time—but I had to allow them to branch off on their own—I trusted them. I didn't care what they saw at a concert, what I cared about was what they did, and they did nothing wrong," Todd explained to me as a proud papa should. Todd understands it. He showcases leadership at its highest level.

Back in 1984 no one was thinking about the 40th anniversary. Not a single person in attendance that night was saying, gee I can't wait till 2024—for in the moment, it was all about Van Halen. It was about *Jump*, guitar solos, beating the heck out of a bass and lighting a gong on fire—I know for a fact, no was thinking about leadership or mentors. All we were thinking about was getting to first base with a girl, *MTV*, VH and maybe *Columbia House* 1 cent cassette's—Jimmy explains the moment clearly for a 2024 perspective, on leadership. "In the moment I didn't think about what my dad did. I didn't think about it, like I think about it now. Man, I can't believe how lucky I was, still to this day—If I can turn out half as good as my dad, then I am doing something right." What an honor for the oldest child, to say that of his father.

As an adult we look back at significant moments that we can recount when a word is spoken—that word is leadership. The minute I was speaking about leadership with Mr. Myres and trying to walk back with him to forty years ago. He opened with a funny story that took place earlier than the Van Halen concert. 1979, and taking multiple kids to see *The Muppet Movie*. Mr. Myres was tasked with looking after eleven kids at the movie—"All holding hands, no other parents would go—I was snaking my way, each kid in hand, from the parking lot to the theatre." Mr. Myres went on to say, "I was the driver and the chaperone, I was there to lookout for the kids." Sound familiar to 1984? Absolutely it does—Five years separated the two events, yet here he was tasked once again with being a leader. Authoritative, in control, as if overseeing a chain-gang, and he did it without complaining—he openly said yes, sure, no problem, I'll do it—as quickly as others asked, he was quicker in his response of showing the way for others to lead. As his son Jimmy describes him, "My dad is a rock star."

With eight children of his own, how he was able to be involved in everything by today's standards, is completely unfathomable—"Five boys and three girls, my dad was always involved with our family." Jimmy said to me with a massive smile on his face, sheer amazement came over him when he was explaining that statement to me—almost in shock of how much his dad means to him, what his dad means to his whole family, and what his dad meant to us kids back in 1984—he was always there. Now that is a tip of the cap to a true leader. For a son to share his feeling about his parent, true unconditional love.

It didn't stop there, Jimmy went on to share a few more insider reflections of his dad, that I had to put in here—for leadership is needed more than ever—"I don't know how my mom and dad did it—mentally and physically it had to be exhausting, and he had to help all the kids with homework." Mr. Myres was not a one-man band, he and his wife Barb are a true beacon for others to follow—raising eight children was not easy, but they found a way, they both were committed, they both were supportive of all their children and they both are true soulmates in a thriving and loving family. Jimmy popped in another piece that truly puts into context what Mr. Myres is to him, and hundreds of kids (grown adults now) around Anderson Twp. "My dad is a dedicated soccer head, he coached my soccer teams, when I started at seven—and was a part of every single kid growing up, in some way of playing soccer—from the backyard to assistant coach, to head coach, to helping special need kids." A dad is a coach, a dad is a leader, and a dad also is a chaperone—all tied up together. Mr. Myres has that edge, and I thank him for it.

Sitting down with Mike, the topic of his dad came up—having spoken on Van Halen, the concert, the van, our childhood memories. Mike explained a side of Mr. Myres that we all saw. The leadership values that come with the title dad. "My dad said, if you ever need a ride, if you ever are in a bad spot, you call me, and I will come pick you up." "Did you ever take him up on that?" I replied. "Sure, I did. I can't remember the occasion, but in my youth and high school days I can remember dad coming over, as a matter of fact, (Mike laughing now) I was thirty-years-old, out at a bar, and I phoned Dad around 1:30 in the morning. Dad, can I get a ride? I think he regretted offering that comment up that day, but Dad jumped out of bed, and picked me up." The Chaperone, and the driver was at the ready for Mike, and for that matter all his kids. In his heart, I know had I called Mr. Myres up, he would have picked me up too, or any of Mike's friends, he was the family AAA.....Still to this day, his willingness to pick the kids up anywhere, anytime is present. "I am now my dad. I told my kids don't drive drunk. (Stevie Wonder would be so proud) I will come and get you, just like my dad." Servant Leader is in Mike's blood, for it has been passed down to the next generation and guess what? Mike's kids feel that skill, feel that unconditional love and they will embrace that tool and do the same thing. Dad was there for me....

In the cop chapter, Eddie tells Skip, "No, I want you to bring your kid." That is a testament to Skip's qualities. It is what they call, the "Halo Effect"—which means, the tendency for an impression created in one area to influence opinion in another area. Leadership > Cop—in this case, Skip's leadership qualities were greater than his Cop qualities, thus allowing Eddie to see the true leader in Skip, instead of just an everyday, detail Cop. Skip had a quality to his actions which not only radiated from what Chris, me and all my buddies could see—but Eddie and all Van Halen witnessed too—thus creating a human connection, and just fulfilling his job requirements. Skip was plussing the occasion. Instead of an A, he was giving an A++++++. Skip was just being Skip. Giving a little more than was required, thus reaping the benefits of being backstage with Van Halen— more to follow in the next chapters.

"My dad is a superhero; he meets the criteria for that!"
—Jimmy Myres

Mr. and Mrs. Myres. Leadership was seen through the eyes of Barb, long before 1984.

MEMORIES...
LAST FOREVER

I remember as a kid how important the photo albums were; they were fully protected, and we had at least ten of them. They were full of photos and memories of my parents, my brother and me. On my fiftieth birthday I was given a photo album by my mom. It was filled with old photos, and photos I had not seen in a long time. It was clear to me how time, effort, and love went into this special gift. Smack in the middle of the album was my confirmation photo, with my wife Gina, Mike Myres, Todd Zimmerman and Chris Berger. Other photos were of my mom and dad and me, my brother, sports including the famous IHM baseball team. We were amazing. Some of my soccer teams. Man, we were good, and so many other pictures. Those photos are tangible items. I can pick them up, I can pass them around, I can look at them forever.

The Polaroid camera and the Kodak drive-up window booth were so popular in the 70s and 80s. I can still recall riding in our station wagon, going to the drive-up window, and getting photos with my mom. That night in 1984, there were no photos taken, there was not a single glimpse into that night other that all our memories of that night, or so I thought. My memory that night is still a little foggy. Sitting down with Mike and speaking of memories, he shared with me, that he did indeed sneak in a camera. The resolution was not that high, the quality was just terrible, and the photo was as blurry as if he was fifteen-sheets to the wind. The catch is, no matter how poor they are by today's standards, Mike captured has that image...both physically and mentally. Unfortunately, Mike has no idea where those pictures ended up, because he no longer has them in his possession. Today it is so simple, use the IPhone, snap, post on social media, and it is saved forever. The difference is, the excitement level of photos is diminishing, unless it's a very special photo, such as a graduation photo, or wedding photo—but everyday photos, well you click and there it is. The anticipation of seeing the photos is not as glamours as it used to be.

What I do have, is a memory bank full of images of that night. I can still see Eddie jamming, still hear Todd doing his Eddie Murphy impersonation, and Mr. Myres standing next to me with wax in his ears. Other memories kick in too, like riding our bikes, spending the night at each other's houses, having birthday parties, and going swimming.

Road trips are a part of family life. Chris has been married for a long time by today's standards...Outstanding Chris and Molly...but like all families, small talk fades away and the radio comes on. When Van Halen comes on the radio, what do you think of? Chris' reaction was instantaneous, the first thing he remembers the minute he recognizes the song, is the concert on that Friday night. It's funny that we reflect on a moment, instantly upon recognizing a Van Halen song, Chris is taken back to 1984. "Surreal"—as Chris states.

"As a father you want to create memories for your kids, this is a memory that he will have forever, and I do too. What meant the most to me, was not me meeting Van Halen and being back there, but having an experience that my son truly enjoyed and will never forget," Skip said. "To see Chris that happy, that joyous, and I was right there with him. It was a powerful father-son moment." Mr. Berger nailed it. It was not about the band; it was about the bond between a father and son. As morbid as it sounds, the day Skip passes away, his son Chris will have so many positive memories of him. Yet, when words like, concert, band, backstage, autographs, and of course Van Halen are spoken that mental photograph of him with his dad will instantly shine through—without any cognitive reasoning to it, as quickly as you can say 1-2-3, Chris will be taken back to 1984.

In speaking with Mr. Berger about memoires lasting forever, he mentions the age of reason. He describes it as the age when one has thought go into an event. It could be a first communion, a first kiss, or a first mixer party at school. He went on to say, "When Chris was twelve and you guys were all the same age, that seems to be the age that you can remember everything." What is hilarious about that comment, is that we all were in the seventh grade, in row ten, at the Van Halen concert. In interviewing all the guys, their recollections of the events that transpired were almost the same. We all remember Autograph, Van Halen, then from there each guy goes into more graphic detail as to what he remembered—Little snippets here and there.

Van Halen, who in the hell are those folks? It's a Friday night, I don't want to drive or chaperone kids, this is my favorite day of the week, and I am using it for myself—or whatever reason dads choose to not get involved. Not in their wheelhouse, nothing in common with the boys or the band. This is not ABBA, nor The Kinks—no way I'll spend my Friday with a bunch of crazed teenagers at the concert. We all know dads that seemed to never get involved, or be involved, unless it was of their choosing. Looking back 40 years, a band that is in the Hall of Fame, a band with four guys that anyone in the industry can rattle off. Yet, parents seem to find an out, the ones that thought they were too important to participate in their kids' lives. It's not about the band (it is now, they are world famous) but in the moment, we have to stop and understand that this moment is a one and done, it can never be recaptured or re-experienced, once it's done, it is done. So, to have your dad or mom be involved, that is an unbeatable memory. Sure, sometimes it's not cool to have your folks tag along, but as Jimmy states, "Lucky as hell, how many people never got to experience a concert with their dad. I didn't take it for granted, just lucky." Jimmy and Mike looking back to 1984, understand that their dad was thrilled to attend, thrilled to be there with them, and thrilled to be there with their friends.

To open this chapter, I spoke of photo albums, which capture our memories forever in an image, and become talking points for family and friends. That's why every phone has a camera. We love to take pictures, in essence it is a measure of proof of what took place. We must snap it, selfie it, group photo it up, or just take a picture of something awe-inspiring, motivating, intriguing, and moving. No matter how we do it, we just seem to take photos. We all love it. That is what the Rock & Roll Hall of Fame is, in one form or another. It is an opportunity to view and take pictures of memorabilia of bands that we love and cherished growing up as kids. Jimmy explains, "My wife Lesa took me to the Rock & Roll Hall of fame for my birthday. I loved it from the moment I saw the big guitar. We were there for hours and hours, and I could go back again." The writing is on the wall, as the saying goes. Jimmy and millions experience the RockHall for different reasons. But Jimmy as well as I experienced the Van Halen exhibit for what it was, to celebrate this awesome band. It seems like all I did was point, explain, laugh, and recall as if a photo album was sitting on my lap. As Jimmy walked the halls, he was pointing, reading, listening, and experiencing music like he had in the past and today. He was in the moment, thus capturing the memories with Lesa, explaining concerts he had seen with his buddies, with all us guys, and his dad too. AWESOME!!!! Jimmy went on to share, "It really hit home, my wife was with me, and we were looking at the Beatles exhibit, and she and I had seen Paul McCartney in concert—he was completely badass.," Jimmy said. They connected with the exhibit right in front of them, just like Van Halen—this time, they were in the moment together.

To experience life, we must go out and about. I hear people say, oh there is nothing to do in this town, this city, or this community—one must venture off, one must get out and about to create memories, experiences, and to feel alive. Music is that avenue. Look up concerts in your area, I don't mean headline events, I mean local artists, local coffee shop performers. All big artists were small once.

I sat down with Mike and asked him this question, "What does Van Halen music mean to you?" He was quick on the draw, and it was not even high noon. He said, "Van Halen brings back memories of yesteryear, the minute I hear one of the older songs on the radio or through *Spotify*." Yesteryear. What does that even mean? The past is the past, it is gone forever. Yet as Mike alluded to, it takes him back to a time of innocence, a time of attempting new concepts, new outings, making new friends, moving on to high school, getting his driver's license, driving to school dances, etc. Memories that Mike can correlate with music, and in this case, Van Halen.

Memory—two weeks before interviewing Mike, not even knowing I would ask him to draw the Van Halen logo, which is at the beginning of the book. Mike drew on his inner Picasso and created this logo on the back window of a van. Notice the flames we talked about earlier.

Jimmy Myres at the Rock & Roll Hall of Hall. (2016)

Concerts—Past, Present and Future

Van Halen was beyond anything I could expect or describe in a first concert—loud, booming, #1 hit, fast, entertaining, creative, packed house, and I was there at thirteen with all of my buddies. It was impactful to say the least, yet so satisfying and so overwhelming as a young man. The scenery, the stage, the arena, the fans, the girls, it was an eye-opening experience. It was *MTV* in person, and I was with my classmates, teammates, and parents I looked up to.

After Van Halen concert, I didn't attend another concert for some time. Each year at IHM we had an end of school year bash, and the band Elaine and The Biscaynes played, or sometimes The Raisins, but I didn't see a band live and on tour for a few years till I got my driver's license. My mom was an interior decorator for a major paint supplier in Cincinnati, and the owners had season tickets to all the concerts at Cincinnati Garden. In 1987 I obtained my driver's license, and my first car was a 1977 gold Volkswagen Rabbit. It had a hand crank moonroof, and hand crank windows, but the thing was I did not have a cassette player in the car. That Christmas in 1987, I got the ultimate gift. I got a new car stereo, and my uncle installed it for me—now I was off to the races. I could drive to school, baseball practice, football practice, and run around with my buddies in style. I now had a cassette player in the car, so Van Halen was right there with me. I was jamming, but I still had not been to another concert. I was seventeen years old, football and high school, sports and of course lifting weights was taking center stage, for I thought I would be the next Arnold Schwarzenegger. Additionally, I had the best job as a cashier at the local convenient store in the neighborhood, so free time was very limited.

My brother at the time was fifteen, and of course he was jamming on his guitar. He was in a band called AS IS, and he was taking piano lessons. We were at complete opposite ends when it came to personality types. One night Mom said to me, "I have free tickets to see George Thorogood." Sure enough, it was two tickets, so my brother and I took the drive over to see him and his band at the Gardens. That was my second concert. We were up and off to the right of the floor, about three-quarters back from the stage in the standard arena seats, with the wooden backs—and I had fun, don't get me wrong, it was great to be there with my brother, but it was not Van Halen. Sure, *Bad to the Bone* was great, but it wasn't *Jump*. Sure, George's guitar playing was lively, but it was not Eddie Van Halen. Sure, George could sing, but it was not David Lee Roth hitting those tunes. Sure, the drummer did well, but it was not Alex. And the bassist, I can't even remember him, well he was no Michael Anthony. Then Mom got a few more tickets and I got to see Bad Company at the Gardens, as well. That was it for me, I didn't see any other concert until I was a freshman in college at the University of Cincinnati, when my co-workers at Convenient Food Mart all decided we should go and see Jimmy Buffett. I took them up on it, and it was fun, tons of drinking, tons of dancing, but it was not as cool as seeing Van Halen back in 1984.

I judged every concert experience against Van Halen in 1984. I judged them on their stage presence, their enthusiasm, and the entertainment value I was receiving. I had just been introduced to customer service at Convenient Food Mart. My dad was in sales, so he would explain value to me. It was Van Halen that reeled me in to grasp the concept of what a band can offer their fans. I was comparing every single performance to Van Halen; it was as if no other band could compare to the level of stage presence that Van Halen gave me when I was thirteen years old. The other bands had to really blow me out of the water. Sometime later after Buffett, I took my brother to see Bob Dylan. Boring! I knew his songs, but to watch a guy just mumble while playing a guitar, was truly boring. He was not Van Halen. Where was the jumping around, and the massive guitar solo? Why wasn't the bass being thrown around? Where were all the screaming girls? Where were the lighters in the air with the flames? Where was the value in that concert? There I was comparing Van Halen to Bob Dylan. To me Bob was so off the current scene. I was not a flower child, my parents were not at Woodstock, all I wanted to do was rock 'n' roll. As Dewey Finn (Jack Black) said in *School of Rock*, "One great rock concert can change the world." Van Halen gave us that performance. On a side note, at least I got to see Bob Dylan.

The Who were always on in my brother's room. Pete Townsend, Roger, Keith, and John were always on, and I liked The Who very much. I saw them in Indianapolis in 2005 for the first time, so they were old. Sitting there in Bankers Life Arena, I was literally sitting in my seat the whole time. Where was the stage performance? Why weren't they running around I thought—but this was 2005, not 1975—they were older, it was great, but it was not Van Halen. That has always been my problem in seeing bands, and that is why I have not been to more than twenty concerts in my lifetime. Sure, I will go and have fun, but I am always comparing the bands to Van Halen, and that *1984* experience. I am judgmental. I am easily bored when not entertained. I have walked out of plays at intermission. I have left baseball games before the seventh inning stretch. I have left many things when I just was not blown away. The older I get, the easier it is for me to become bored with poor entertainment value—

$12.50 was the price of the ticket in '84. Today that easily would be $1000.00 for row 10 to see any major band in person. So $12.50 was the best deal I had ever received. Think about it, $12.50 for 90 minutes of a concert, plus we got to see an opening act too, Autograph. They played for say thirty minutes—so for two hours I was stimulated from start to finish, and it only cost me $6.25 an hour to watch this.

Reliving an experience never fulfills the original experience. We try to live or recapture a moment that we loved, and it is never as fulfilling as the first time. We take the same vacations to the same spots and hit up the same restaurants each time—boring. That is what Van Halen did for me, even though I never saw them again. Yes, I bought their music. Yes, I followed them, but it was because of the four of them giving me my money's worth, that seeing other concerts and bands became a huge let down. I often wonder if I would have seen a different band first, if they would have given me the same feelings, the same enjoyment, the same positive memories as Van Halen did. I always say no, to try and compare is not fair to me or the imaginary bands. Van Halen was the coolest band in the 80s and I was there to see them perform and perform they did. I cannot thank them enough.

Concerts to me personally are still fun, but as of writing this it has been over two years since I have been to a concert. I saw Heart and Jon Jett with my wife and daughter, and that same summer we also saw The Who. Both concerts were good, but no Van Halen. The thing I remember about The Who concert in Noblesville, Indiana was running into my high school classmate Mike Engelkamp. I also remember watching my teenage daughter experience an outdoor venue for the first time and rocking out to Joan Jett. Maybe I should go see a current concert, but like I said, I will judge them in every single category a band has to offer, from sound, to lighting, to entertainment value, to parking, to clarity, to zest and pizzaz, to memorable experience.

In an article, written by staff writer Ruben Castaneda for *US News & World Report* titled *6 Reasons Going to Concerts Is Good for Your Health*. The following list appears:

1. stress reduction
2. pain relief
3. a sense of connection and community
4. an opportunity to reflect on your life
5. good exercise
6. a sense of well-being

"Michael, I'll do a shot with you, if you can?" Those are the words Chris Berger said to Michael Anthony back in August 1993, during the *Balance Tour*, at Riverbend Music Center in Cincinnati, Ohio, on the banks of the Ohio River. Chris and a few of his friends went to see Van Halen with Sammy Hagar, which turned into another night of unconquerable memories. Before the concert even started, Chris had access to right of the stage, with a fellow VIP holder. Chris not even having a backstage pass, found himself literally backstage among the crew, and the dressing rooms. In Chris' words, "I slipped out of the VIP area, nothing but doors and doors and more doors. I turned the knob of a few, but they were locked. So, I tried a few more with the determination to see Van Halen—luckily, one was unlocked. 'Holy Shit, you are Michael Anthony!!!!' So here I was at twenty-three years old, thinking like I was twelve again attending my first concert. Only this time I was an adult, with a kid's mindset that I'm going to see the band. And there was Michael, sitting at a table with a bottle of Jack Daniels. I said, 'Hey Mike, I am a huge fan.' Michael Anthony replied, 'Want to do a shot with me?' 'Sure thing,' I said. And the two of us did a shot—I didn't know what to do next, so I said, 'Thanks. Are you opening with *Unchained*?' 'Sorry buddy, the set list is final, and unfortunately, we are not playing *Unchained*.' Michael told me, with a look of bewilderment, as if to say who is this guy." Mission complete, as in the movie *The Dirty Dozen*.....target acquired, with precise accuracy. Chris had a drink with a Hall of Famer....BINGO!!!!!!! One Van Halen concert was not enough for Chris. Chris shared with me that he had seen Van Halen fifteen times. The first time was in 1984 and the last time was in 2015, with Diamond Dave and Wolfgang. They even played *Unchained*.

Not just once, or twice, but fifteen times Chris has witnessed Van Halen. David Lee Roth, Eddie Van Halen, Michael Anthony, Alex Van Halen, Sammy Hagar, Gary Cherone, and Wolfgang Van Halen. Fifteen times is a lifetime in the rock business, moreover that is over thirty hours of viewership of the iconic band. I would say Chris is an expert when it comes to Van Halen, or at the very least a mega-fan. Chris has a twenty-two-year-old daughter, and Chris has never been to a concert with her. She has been to five or six concerts. I asked Chris what he thought when she asked to go to her first concert. He answered, "I was all for it at first, then I heard the band she was going to see, weeeeeellllll okay. It brought up the trigger of our first concert." Chris knew it was not an issue, but if he didn't hesitate, he wouldn't be a good parent. All of us are uneasy about our kids venturing off to experience a first. Chris responded first as a parent, then next as a fellow rock and roller. He couldn't say no, knowing that his parents had said yes. Scared, sure Chris was. He was thrilled his daughter was off to see her first concert.

When is a chaperone no longer a chaperone? The answer is lies within Mr. Myres, and his ability to say yes—his enjoyment of attending concerts took over the title that was blessed upon him. He now was part of the group—from KISS to Van Halen to numerous other concerts, Mr. Myres was part of the inner circle. The proof was in the pudding. Not only did he take his boys, but he also took his girls. "If I am going to see a soccer game, I am not there to see the kids, I am there to see the soccer match. I liked them [Van Halen] a lot better than seeing other concerts I took the kids to." Mr. Myres went on to say, "Some concerts I attended, felt like I was watching paint dry." Apples to oranges, comparing venues to each other, I am sorry to say this but when you have seen the best, and you follow that up with a weaker concert, you will always have a letdown. It is like Dewey Finn said in *School of Rock*, "God of Rock, thank you for this chance to kick ass. We are your humble servants. Please give us the power to blow people's minds with our high voltage rock. In your name, we pray, Amen." That is exactly what happened to Mr. Myres. He was literally blown away by Van Halen. From start to finish Van Halen gave him his money's worth. Then he found himself at another concert, looking at his watch, asking himself should I have used a darker blue?

Girls just want to have fun too you know; it can't be all about the boys in the Myres family. Experiencing a concert with his daughter was a wonderful moment for Mr. Myres. He sat there at the table giving me a play by play, as if the concert happened yesterday. "My daughter Ann took me to see Arlo Guthrie at the Aronoff Center, in downtown Cincinnati. I can play *Alice's Restaurant* over and over in my head. It was good, he is quite the entertainer. Ann was the youngest person in the audience, and everyone had grey hair except for Ann. It was a memorable moment." Mr. Myres asked me, "Do you know how many times you can play that song from Cincinnati to Rochester, New York?" He answered his own question really quick, "Twenty times, the minute it was over I would hit repeat—twenty times, Jimmy…. What a super concert that was for us."

How many times have you been to a concert with a family member only to rehash that moment ten to fifteen years later? Unbeatable, the power of music has on us all, even if you hated a band so much in high school, that one song will trigger that one positive moment that you can recollect from your past. It is the product of association, and it works every single time. No matter the artist, no matter how much you made fun of them in years past, they will come to a small concert hall in your town, and you will go see them. The very band you frowned upon, now you like. The very song you just could not stand on *Casey's Top 40*, you will want to go and see them. Do it, create that memory. It's funny that the music I never listened to in high school and college, are just a few of the concerts I have seen over the past ten years. So, go for it.

As we sat there talking over breakfast, Mike and I began speaking about venues and our own kids. He asked who I had taken my daughter to see, and thus snowballed right into Mike's memory. Which kicked into overdrive about his recollection of his first concert with his kids. "My wife and I took our boys to their first concert, My Chemical Romance at Riverbend Music Center." Small talk faded away, and a positive memory came over Mike, one that his wife, his boys and he will never forget. A family moment that all will remember forever. Long after Mike is gone, his boys will have that image captured in their memories forever. Like Skip said earlier in the book, "It was the experience with Chris that made that night so special." Mike's boys too, have that memory, as well as his wife. But, collectively as a family they all can hold that evening sacred. Words like romance and chemical will instantly trigger their subconscious.

People say, I am too busy to see a concert. I don't have the money to see a concert. Yet, they have all the streaming services in the world through their TV. That is the difference today versus the 60s, 70s, 80s and 90s. We didn't have *YouTube* to watch a concert, nor did we have *Pandora* to stream our favorite tunes. We had to catch a glimpse on *MTV*, which was hit or miss, or catch the hour where we can listen to our category and hope that our song will be on. We had to listen to the radio or catch them in concert. Jimmy shared with me that he has seen Van Halen seven times, lucky number seven. There was no luck to it. It was just that Jimmy tried to get blown away seven times, for he loves the band, enjoys their stage presence, loves the songs, and the jamming. To be repeat a customer like Chris and Jimmy are, speaks volumes to what every single business wants—repeat customers. Too bad there wasn't a reward membership punch card for Chris, Todd, and Jimmy. They would have earned a free all-expense paid trip to Bali, Indonesia by now. They both would have been on their second punch card and would have received a free fill up on pump #5 for life. The points generated might have even put Chris' kid through college......

I have to make up for lost time. We all know folks over the age of fifty who seem to be cramming everything in their life right now, for fifty seems to be right past that mid-life crisis and right as your *AARP* card comes in the mail. They are trying to make up for what they have lost or were not involved in. They may be drinking, hitting the bar scene, vacationing, and now even attending concerts. Bob Buford wrote a great book called *Halftime*, about hitting the halftime in your life, with regret in this first half, thus overcompensating in the second half. That is what I see and hear all the time. Folks trying to do more and see more to make up for what they didn't experience in their youth. Money could have been an issue, time, or whatever other excuse we give. The point is the time will never be perfect for anything, therefore we have to say yes a little bit more often when it comes to youth trying stuff out for the first time. That is what all us guys did, and what our parents allowed us to do, we all had jobs in high school, no one was born with a silver spoon. We earned what we obtained, and we thrived at getting out and seeing the world, even if it was ten miles down the road at a concert. We did it! Jimmy put it in perspective very well, "Concerts are so expensive now. We paid around $400 dollars to see the Foo-Fighters. Today I am picky, before I got out of high school, I'd say I had been to over thirty outings by graduation." He nailed it. If it was $12.50 for row ten in 1984, and $400 dollars today, what is going to be in another forty years? $15,000 dollars? The price of a ticket is everything, but in forty years no one will ask if you were you in the top row or the front row. No one will care. The catch is, we can pay $50 for top level seats, so do it! Take those kids, take those kids and their friends.... The best seats are meaningless years afterwards, the key is you were there and that is the meaning of the concert. The best seats do not create the best memories all the time, and vice versa the worst seats don't create the worst memories. Being in attendance is better than sitting at home wishing and hoping you had the perfect view. Most concerts are about the experience and the friends you share it with. As quick as the lead singer says, "Thank you Cincinnati, see you next time," the show will be over.

"My wife and I love live music," Jimmy says. Coming from a guy who had been to over thirty concerts before high school graduation, that resonates with so many people across the United States and the world. If you were lucky enough to grow up in the 70s and 80s, it seems as if every single band that we hear today on the local oldies station, who are in the Hall of Fame were on tour then, year after year, and it seemed to never stop. Traveling baseball teams was not a thing, and all year around conditioning was not talked about. Summer was summer. You had a fun job, could hang out with friends, and enjoy life. Jimmy lived and breathed that, as well as Chris, Mike, Todd, and me—baseball, pool parties, sleepovers, movie nights, hitting up Blockbuster Video, and of course MTV. We were fortunate in Cincinnati to have three concert venues, Riverbend Music Center, Cincinnati Gardens, and of course Riverfront Coliseum. So, concerts were all over town. This was no different than any other major city, as there were numerous concerts to choose from. The point is, rapid fire from all directions, a constant barrage of musicians to see. We chose wisely, but we chose often, and we loved every single minute of it. No Regrets!

We all have that one concert in us that we wished we would have seen. It could have been Queen, Van Halen, KISS, The Beatles, Elvis, The Animals, Cream, or even The Firm (Paul Rodgers, Chris Slade, Jimmy Page, and Tony Franklin.) But, we hesitated, we said tomorrow, next time they come around. However, to buy tickets, and then not have the ability to see, them that's another thing, as Jimmy shares, "One concert I never made it to was The Who in 2022, at TQL Stadium here in Cincinnati. I bought tickets, but something came up, and I could not attend. I bought two tickets for that concert for Lesa and me. I had wanted to see them for a long time, but we never made it." I would say Jimmy had a justifiable reason not to attend. As the pilot says, take care of yourself first, then help others. Jimmy needed to take care of himself, for he has many concerts still to attend. And who knows, The Who's reunion tour was in 1989, and here Jimmy missed them in 2022, so they will be back Jimmy. No worries, buddy. Here is the kicker, instead of letting the tickets go to waste, he gave them to Mike, therefore Mike got to see The Who— keeping it in the Myres family—very cool.

To see Van Halen in 1984 was one for the ages, as Jim Nantz would say. To experience them in other cities, well that would only be a pipedream as we were all under the age of eighteen. None of us knew what was ahead in the music scene, that cassette tapes would surpass the 8-track, and CDs would surpass cassette tapes. But concerts, love of live music, and the buy-in to Van Halen became stronger and stronger as noted by Jimmy and Chris.

After that 1984 night we wondered, what are the odds of seeing Van Halen as buddies again? Could we? We were about to start eighth grade, high school was on the horizon, and we were about to go our separate ways—the real world was starting to set in. Sadly, it never happened, my fingers are still crossed for the future. Having left the concert on a high (just joking Mrs. Zimmerman,) Todd knew at thirteen that he would see Van Halen again. Todd, Chris, and Jimmy mounted an internal Van Halen Fan Club—having seen then multipule times and in Todd's case, he has seen Van Halen thirteen times—Holy Cow!!!!! Thirteen times, the power of one great concert is relevant. It's moving, inspiring, and it brings out the kid in us. As stated earlier, sometimes revisiting an event can take away the blissful feelings of the first encounter. This is not true for Todd. He has not only saw them in Cincinnati (Riverbend Music Center, The Cincinnati Gardens and U.S Bank Arena,) but he also got to enjoy them in San Diego, CA and in Long Beach, CA. "Every time Van Halen came to Cincinnati, I saw them," Todd explained to me as he rattled off that list. He loves the entertainment value, loves the band, and loves everything about attending a Van Halen concert. He is not a one show pony, at this point he is part of the band, not really, but with that many times attending I would say he was. In other words, if a concert lasts two hours, Todd has spent twenty-six hours of his life witnessing and watching Van

Halen. That is one whole day, plus two hours. He would be a season ticket holder, if there was such an item with Van Halen.

To get back to '84, how would we all see Van Halen again? It's hard to get everyone together, but as Todd and Chris prove, anything worth doing, you will find a way. Todd continues, "Chris Berger and I went to a Van Hagar concert together, many years later. Yes, with the lead singer Sammy Hagar." Todd and Chris made it back to their roots to see them as a team, just like in '84. Sure, there was no van, no Gardens, but to be there and talk and feel the vibe as young adults, that is truly something special. Two Van Halen concerts with a friend from grade school, both whose first concerts were Van Halen is pure awesomeness.

As it shows, Todd is a massive live concert advocate. He is an evangelist for Van Halen. Spreading the word for all to hear, as far as Todd could travel—Ohio to California, Todd has those bases covered. But there is one artist that Todd has seen even more times. Can you guess who???????? Hint, he was in a soap opera, with the Initials G.H. Can you guess it? Rick Springfield... "There is only one artist that I have seen more than Van Halen, and that is Rick Springfield. I have seen him seventeen times," Todd went into a pure pandemonium of laughter. As a matter of fact, Todd and his wife Tosh have seen Rick three times together. Now to take this even higher, Chris Berger and Todd have seen Rick Springfield two times together. I am now laughing as I write this. The great approach Todd has to these concerts is, you will never catch him at the same theatre, watching is favorite artist. Todd is selective, taking in the ambience and the characteristics of new stages.

Chris has seen numerous concerts as well—Metallica, Godsmack, Beastie Boys, Foo Fighters, Rob Zombie, Run DMC, Disturbed, Korn, Pearl Jam, Alice in Chains, Kid Rock, and the bands go on and on for what seems like an eternity (we would need a bigger book.) What is captivating about these bands is the vivid memory Chris continually plays over and over upon entering the venues. Chris explains, "I am instantly taken back to that Friday night in 1984, at the Gardens, and all I do is smile." That testimony lives and breathes because Van Halen gave him the performance of his lifetime, which thus created a concert goer for life. Bands thank him, *Ticketmaster* thanks him, S*tubhub* thanks him, and of course ALL the beer vendors thank him.

To say you're a Van Halen fan is one thing, to attend a Van Halen concert is another, and to purchase Van Halen albums, posters, wallets is another thing too—you set yourself apart from the other fans. Todd and Chris are raving fans. Now to set the bar even higher with Todd, I know it's not a competition, but Todd needs to be recognized as the true leader of Van Halen fans. "I got to see Wolfgang, with Van Halen, when he took

Michael Anthony's place on tour." To see Eddie live on stage back in '84, then to see his son perform live too, that is just incredible. "There is a sound to Wolfgang, and it is really good," Todd shared as he played the air guitar, intertwining Eddie and Wolfgang in the same jam. Todd knows his bands. It gets even better, I don't know how much more there is to top what Todd has seen, but here we go— "I have seen The Circle numerous times, and there was Sammy Hagar and Michael Anthony in the band, and they were amazing." Todd has a batting average of 1000. I don't know anyone who could top this—if you, the reader can top Todd, then please email me and let me know. I would love to hear your story and share your story with the guys and other readers.

Jimmy stated that he had been to over thirty concerts before graduating high school—that is a ton. Chris has seen Van Halen fifteen times, and Todd has seen them thirteen times—so how many concerts do think Todd has seen altogether at fifty-three years old????? "Seeing Van Halen in '84, is what turned me on to live music. I have been to well over one-hundred and fifty concerts," Todd chuckled, as he gasped for air, having been winded as hell explaining to me all these details, but it was one concert that changed it all for Todd. "Van Halen could put out a new song today, and I will be just as excited today as I was back in 1984." Now that my friends, is noteworthy.

Earlier in the book, Jimmy shared with me that he had been in a garage band. No real structure to it, no band name. Just a few friends that would assemble and play a few tunes. As of interviewing him in 2022, he shared that he had just purchased a brand new Fender Stratocaster. To understand the power of music, in the 80s Jimmy was in a band mimicking the very bands he would listen to, and the very bands he witnessed in person. In 2022, Jimmy obtained a new guitar, now that is powerful. He still has the love and passion of a striking a chord, and the feeling of being a part of the band.

Just imagine if Todd's parents would have told him no back in 1984, but in 1985 told him yes to a totally different concert, different location, different friends, different chaperone— would Todd be a fan of Van Halen? We will never know, but the point is Todd's parents, as did mine, Mike's and Chris' said yes—thus allowing us to be introduced to rock 'n' roll, and Van Halen, and *JUMP*…. I asked Todd about going to concerts with his kids, and what he said to them? Todd shared with me, that he instantly said yes, "I took my daughter Kelsea to her first concert, Britney Spears. We had front row seats, she was twelve. To make it even better, my sister Tara got us backstage passes. Then the following year at age thirteen, I took her to see Britney again, this time second row seats." Second row—only eight rows better than 1984, and Todd got to experience her first concert with her. How cool is that a memory that she will have forever, all because Todd was told "YES" forty years ago. The power of one word, it can change everything for a teenager.

Twelve and thirteen, still so young, yet Todd had to let her go and experience life for herself, still under his wings, yet giving her wings to fly, prosper, and see the world through her own eyes, instead of his. Todd, in father fashion, explained when he let his daughter go to the concert— "Just like us, I had let my daughter go with seven other girls, with another chaperone to see the Jonas Brothers. I was not there." That night Todd felt like our parents back in 1984, waiting up to hear all about it, for they weren't there. Todd trusted her, knew the chaperone, and he knew his daughter was in good hands, just like Mr. Myres was to all of us. Another moment came around for Todd in 2022. His daughter and he got to experience another concert together, this time both as adults, when they attended LeAnn Rimes. Todd told me that music really wasn't big in his household growing up, just talk radio. Todd though was sold on live music, thus sharing this with me. "In 2014 I took my parents, with my wife Tosh, to Maroon 5, and Kelly Clarkson was with them. We had the best time. Dad really enjoyed Kelly Clarkson." Diehard passion for live music sums up Todd's personality, and he loves sharing that passion with his wife, kids, and his parents.

"I was in 3rd grade and Dad took Jimmy, myself, and Dave (younger brother) to a KISS concert, and Judas Priest opened for them. I had never heard something so damn loud in my life when KISS took the stage. I was blown away. My ears finally adjusted, but man was that loud," Mike shared this with me about his first concert. Notice who he remembers took him and who he was with, family. Music supplies an outlet where we can grasp the importance of a moment, once we hear the bands name, or an individual song. That hits a chord within us. We instantly have a time-stamped moment. As of writing this, last night May 12, 2023, Mike went to see Brit Floyd at the PNC Pavilion here in Cincinnati with a few of his buddies. Now when a Pink Floyd song comes on, Mike will recall who he was with, where he was, and what an awesome time he had. During the interview with Mike as he shared his first concert of the summer, he instantly chimed in, and said, "I saw ZZ Top last summer at Riverbend Music Center."

We don't have to experience as many venues as Chris, Todd, and Jimmy have, to get our money's worth. One great concert can change everything. "I have only been to one Van Halen concert. Well, I have only been to around twenty concerts in my life," Mike stated—which is now twenty-one and climbing.

Jimmy Myres and his wife Lesa.
Las Vegas, Nevada.

Jim Serger and his wife Gina.
The Vogue—Indianapolis, Indiana.

Todd Zimmerman and his wife Tosh.
Riverbend Music Center—Cincinnati, Ohio.

Chris Berger and his wife Molly.
Rupp Arena—Lexington, Kentucky.
The t-shirt explains the concert they are about to attend.

Skip Berger and his wife Jan.
Riverbend Music Center—Cincinnati, Ohio

Autographs

Autograph and autographs—two for one again that night in 1984...The opening act, we got to see a band that launched a hit that still rings true to this day on the radio waves, but to get autographs well that was not a given going into the concert that night. As we all entered the Gardens, I remember all of us running up to the merchandise stand and grabbing our *1984* Van Halen Tour Guide. It was a must have. Sure, a ticket stub was proof we were there, but to have the actual guide, now that was something else.

There we were in row ten, the Gardens lights at full force, and everyone running around to their seats. When out of know where there was Mr. Berger standing next to us, asking for our tour guides. Without any hesitation whatsoever we all handed them to the right, almost like the offering basket in church, making its way down the pew on Sundays. But this time we were offering them up to the Rock Gods, Van Halen. We all knew that morning that Mr. Berger was working the Van Halen concert. We all knew this because Chris shared with us that his dad was working backstage. how cool. Mr. Berger was standing shoulder to shoulder with David, Michael, Eddie, and Alex, and he was backstage. Unbelievable, there is a chance that all of us guys could get our tour books signed by all of them.

The concert was about to commence, and we never saw our tour books again. Good I say, they would have been ruined, trampled on, beer spilled on them, torn up, who knows what would have happened. The cop knew what to do. He collected them all and protected them with his 9mm backstage. I have zero recollection of being concerned about my tour book. What are the odds that VH would come through? What are the odds that Mr. Berger would come through? 100% Let me repeat that, 100% Mr. Berger came through.

The next morning was Saturday, and I know the autographs were the last thing on my mind, but I wanted my tour book back. Back at school on Monday, Chris Berger had a halo over his head, a glow that could be seen from afar, for he had the Bible of all Bibles in his hand. He had our tour books, and there on full display was four autographs—Alex, Eddie, Michael, and David—OH MY GOD!!!! Mr. Berger surprised us, by taking our tour books and having the guys sign them. All of us were given these sacred scrolls, these precious items, and each of us could not thank Mr. Berger enough. That bus ride home from school was the most rewarding thirty-minute jaunt I had ever been on, because everyone on the bus wanted to see the autographs. They wanted to hear the story and wanted to know about the concert. I know Chris, Mike, and Todd were receiving the same attention. It was if we were being drilled at a Super Bowl press conference, the winning QB under fire, praise, smiles from ear to ear, scratchy voices, the redness of my face, the pats on the back, the cheering and celebration was just so lively.

That afternoon after I watched *Scooby-Doo* on TV, which every kid did the minute they got home, it was always on at 3. When Mom got home from work, I showed her the autographs. She was so happy. Then around 5:30 Dad got home, and I showed him, I am sure his statement was, "Pretty cool." But the one line I remember the most was from my brother, "I would burn those if I were you, they are worthless." Worthless, are you kidding me? Mom got a picture frame for that tour book, for that was a journey of a thousand words—more like a million or infinity of words. That frame was going to go up right on my wall, sure enough my bedroom welcomed Van Halen with open arms.

In November of 2022, while conducting interviews for this book I decided to go and get the autographs appraised. I headed over to Sports Investments Inc. located at 10026 Montgomery Road here in Cincinnati. This place knows their stuff, and even has Pete Rose's red Corvette in the showroom. They have shelf after shelf, display case after case filled with sports memorabilia. I knew I was in the right place, plus they had just purchased all my baseball cards (No one wants those anymore.) While there completing the deal, the owner asked if there was anything else I had of interest to sell. I told him, "I have a signed '84 Van Halen tour book." "Bring it in," he responded. The next day I drove up, and he began to examine the book, eyeglasses on, then off, then he proceeded to pull out a loupe as if my book were a precious diamond. Finally, he said, "This is a hell of a piece. Give me fifteen minutes." With that, he went to the back office, and closed the door behind him. I paced back-and- forth, back-and-forth—then he came out, sweat dripping off his forehead, medical gloves removed, he said, "It's worth $1500 to $2000 dollars." "Holy Shit," I said, "that is crazy—all these years I never would have fathomed that." But the man with a degree in sports memorabilia told me so—therefore, as an expert in the field, I had to take him at his word. "$2000 dollars." He offered, "Would you like to sell it?" I quickly responded, "No way. That is too valuable to me." Not the cash part, but the memory part that the tour book has given to me—the memory of my buddies, Mr. Myres, and Mr. Berger are all wrapped up in that priceless artifact. He went on to share, "That if I knew anyone else who had them, tell them to head on up." I said, "Yes sir, thank you for your time. Thank you for kindness and thanks for making something incredible, that much more remarkable." Priceless—this belongs in a museum.

The minute I got home, I called Mr. Berger and proceeded to explain all about the adventure to the sports card shop. He was shocked, and said, "You have got to call Chris." I did, and Chris about passed out on the phone. $2000 dollars for an artifact that he was fully protecting in his basement. Chris was overwhelmed with joy, for it just heightened that night 1984-fold.

I have sold almost all of my memorabilia, but the two things that I still have on display to this day for all to see are, #1—My Pete Rose rookie jersey, which is signed by him. This was a Christmas gift from parents in 1991. My dad and I went to Dayton, Ohio for a baseball card show to have Pete sign it. That was an excellent trip, that would develop into many more with my dad. #2—The Van Halen tour book with the autographs. I protect these two items with everything I have. They are not replaceable at all—I could probably buy fake ones, or mass-made one, but these two items are 100% authentic, and 100% generate a memory that no one can take away.

As a kid, who was snuck in the backstage door by his dad, Chris states, "Everything was a blur, it seemed like the opening of a roller-coaster, the anticipation, the massive line, which seems never ending, then the ride itself, lasted all of three minutes—it was a blur, pure blur to me at twelve-years-old. I do remember shaking Eddie's hand, and just being in complete awe of him. I shook Michael's, David's, and Alex's too, other than that, those five minutes backstage is fogged over."

"They don't sign autographs." That is what a fellow cop told Skip that night backstage. "Van Halen, they do not sign autographs."—well that was for the other cop, but not for Skip Berger. Skip had no clue; he was not concerned, and he made it happen. When Skip took Chris backstage, Chris notes, "Passing the one-hundred drop dead gorgeous women in the hallway." Chris handed off his *1984* cassette tape sleeve—hoping he would get it signed. Skip said, "I can't believe they signed and gave him all that stuff." Chris received guitar pics, and numerous '84 painter caps. It felt like Christmas morning.

"Surprise, surprise, surprise."—that was Mike's reaction that Monday morning after receiving the autographs. The icing on the cake was Mike also received a guitar pic…"I was in awe. I had no idea we were getting any of this," Mike told me, then continued, "Mr. Berger came through, having the signatures of the band, from the very concert I had just seen, was mind blowing. To have a piece of the actual concert in my possession was just over the top." *Mike, come party with us.* —that is how Mike's tour book was signed. It was personalized to him. The band knew who Mike Myres was, just maybe they had heard of Mike's piano skills and wanted to hear him play some Beethoven. Well, at least Eddie, David, and Alex did. Michael Anthony didn't sign his book. I like to think Michael Anthony was in such awe of Mike's skill set, that he is the one who addressed the book and wanted to party with Mike so badly, that he forgot to sign it. Stroh's beer, anyone?

Todd had his program framed to protect it from the elements, which was on full display down in his teenage basement party pad. One year Todd had a massive birthday party, and a friend at the time was goofing around and broke the frame, ripping the insides of the program. Leaving only the cover intact. As Todd puts it, "Pure devastation." Todd even goes on further to share, "We haven't spoken since that day."

Jim Serger's *1984* tour book autographed by all the members of Van Halen.
Eddie, top left. Michael, top right.
David, right above the eyes.
Alex, right above the hand with the cigarette in it.

Todd Zimmerman's autographed *1984* tour book.

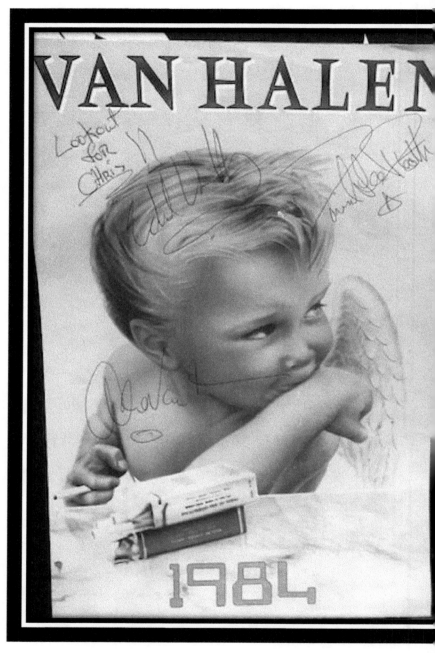

Chris Berger's autographed *1984* tour book—notice it says, "Look out for Chris!!" He is missing Michael Anthony's signature.

Chris Berger's second set of autographs—amazing!
Notice on this one, all the members are present and accounted for.

Chris Berger's third set of autographs that night—truly incredible. What a tribute to Skip Berger. The band respected him enough, to dish out multiple signatures.

Ticket Stubs

Everyone loves ticket stubs. It's like a snow skier that has all the ski lifts attached to their zipper, it's like, "Hey look at me. Look what I have done," as they go down the Black Diamond. I understand saving them. It's like a marathon runner creating a wall with all the medals on display. That is what ticket stubs were back in the day. When I was a young man, I use to collect beer cans. These cans that were given to me by my dad who drank them all. He choose beers he never would drink, just because I needed that can to add to the collection. I had wrap around wooden shelves about ten inches below my ceiling in my bedroom where the cans were on full display. Hey, I too was like, look at all the beer cans I have, that my dad drank—well back in the late 70s and early 80s collecting cans was in.

Ticket stubs are no longer an item to collect, they are not sought after at all. All we do now is download our tickets to our phone, then scan them as we go into the event. BORING!!!! But in 1984, ticket stubs were the proof that you attended an event—World Series, Super Bowl, rock concerts, All-Star Game. We didn't have cell phones back then, nor *Facebook* to tag the location to prove, yes, we were there. Ticket stubs were the memento that one received for attending. The ticket would be ripped in half, half for the venue and the other half for me, the collector.

March 9, 1984—yes, I still have that ticket stub. It is in the picture frame with the Van Halen autographs. It is my stamp of approval that I was there, I was accounted for, and yes, I was present. My Van Halen ticket stub says the date, the row, the section and in bold italics it says *Van Halen*. I have no selfie, and my buddies and I did not take a group photo that night. In '84 there were a ton of rules when entering concert venues, including:

#1 No pictures were allowed to be taken
#2 No video equipment was allowed in the venue
#3 No audio equipment was allowed in

Nowadays all three of these rules are nonexistent because of smart phones. Back in 1984 all you could bring in was a lighter and smokes, and of course girls could bring in a purse—no clear bags were needed. But rules are meant to be broke, which Mike and Chris did that night. They in fact snuck in a camera, and Chris still has the photos he took that night. Mikes are gone, but not forgotten. As a matter of fact, while interviewing Chris and seeing his collection of Van Halen photos there are a few that came from his camera, but totally unrecognizable as to who the photos are of. So blurry, just like Mike's fifteen-sheets to the wind. Proof they were there, but only to themselves. Photos are of the poorest quality.

The very nature of this book, is what each one of us experienced individually and collectively. Like a boulder rolling down a hill, it seemed to gather more speed as each of the guys share their memories. Chris's wife said, "I had never heard that before, in describing that night." This again, is adding fuel to the fire. The massive blaze just keeps getting bigger and bigger upon speaking with the guys. It's hard to fathom how much took place in one evening because there were so many moving parts. Mike having the wits to sneak in a camera, is something for the record books.

Proof, that is what the ticket stub stands for. I was there, I saw them, I was there for the drum solo, the bass solo, and of course for the guitar solo—I was there......I witnessed them, and this ticket is proof that I was indeed in person to watch Van Halen.

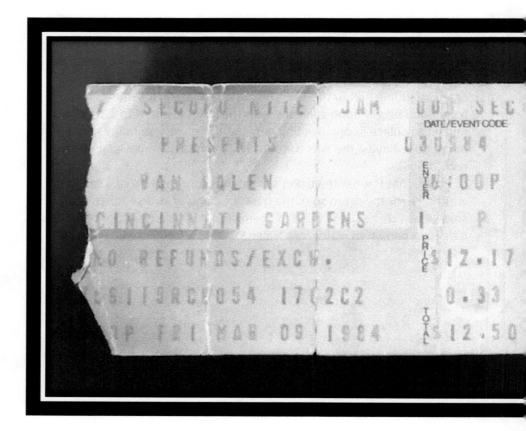

Jim Serger's actual ticket from that night back in 1984.

A ticket stub from that night—Skip gave to Chris.
Chris believes this is a stub of one of the ruffian's that Skip and his crew
had to escort out of the   Gardens. The beat cops had to retain the
ticket, so the punk cold not re-enter.

Jimmy Myres' ticket sleeve.
Saved after all these years.

A ticket stub from that night, which Chris picked up off the floor of The Gardens on the way out.

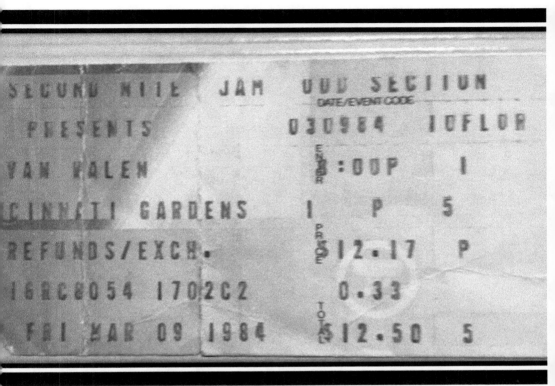

Chris Berger's ticket—but remember, Chris did not have a ticket that night.
So, I am sure this is either, Todd's or Mike's ticket, which ended up in Chris' possession after the festivities that evening.

RP0419   SEC.1   G 39 A   35.00
35.00 FLOOR
3.00   SUNSHINE PRESENTS
SEC.1   VAN HALEN
OPC   1X   FOOD DONATIONS AT DOOR
G   39   RUPP ARENA/LEXINGTON KY
2011000   NO CAMERAS/RECORDERS
25FEB5   WED APR 19 1995 7:30 PM

Chris and Molly's ticket stub from 1995, which correlates to the photo of them. Notice the price of the ticket, $35.00 dollars. Just eleven years earlier we paid $12.50 for our tickets, and we were in Row 10.

RB0813   300   I 324   A   32.5

32.5[2.25 PRK PD-USE EVENT LO

5.0[BUDWEISER CONCERTS

ONVENIENCE CHARGE   VAN HALEN

30[FOOD DONATIONS AT DOOR

OH 35×   RIVERBEND MUSIC CENTER

I 32×   NO CAMERAS/RECORDERS

BOX   SEAT

6MAY5   SUN AUG 13 1995 8:00 PM

Chris Berger's ticket stub from 1995—same year as previous ticket, this time
it was $2.50 cheaper.

Happy Trails

"Happy Trails to you, until we meet again."
--*Happy Trails*, Van Halen.

The journey of growing and learning never stops. We don't get a stop sign at graduation, on our wedding day, or when we retire. *Happy Trails* means, that should keep pursuing more adventures, keep touring the countryside, continue experiencing new lands, and never stop seeing new cities and new bands. That is what the closing song means to me—it means, we will see you again, in the meantime get off your butt and do something. Take up scuba diving, run that marathon, get your CDL, write that book, get that band out of the garage and into a high school gym, do that stand-up comedy routine—whatever it is, go and do it. *Happy Trails*.

Since this book was written, my wife and I have been out to dinner with the guys and their wives. It was not just a one and done. We are keeping the positive vibe going. We just had to reconnect and stay connected, that is what this journey was about. Van Halen—Eddie jumping and spreading his legs. David jumping all over the place like a crazed joker. Alex catching the stage on fire. Michael hitting the chord so loud it vibrated the fillings in my teeth. Those guys would be back in Cincinnati again. They were not a one and done. That is the message Van Halen instilled in us—365 days later there would be a possibility of Van Halen being back in the Queen City. If they toured here, people would come, the house would sell out, because they were in demand.

As a teenager, I didn't understand the power that concert would have on me, because music was not that important. It was all about sports, music was for other people. Boy, was I wrong. As an adult I know Van Halen gave me an appreciation for music, not just live music, but music in general—all because I saw them in person.

In the fall of 1984, the movie *The Terminator* was released, which gave us the famous slogan, "I'll Be Back!!" It is still as prevalent today, as it was back then. From a customer service perspective, it really hit home. In 2021, *New York Times* best-selling author, Shep Hyken wrote the book *I'll Be Back: How to Get Customers to Come Back Again & Again*. As I read that book, Van Halen really hit home for me. Van Halen gave us one of the best nights in the world, thus creating fans forever. One of Shep's takeaways is, "THE HUMAN TOUCH IS ESSENTIAL TO CREATING CUSTOMER LOYALTY." Live and in person, Van Halen gave us the human touch. We were thirty feet away from the stage, we have signed tour books, pictures of the band, guitar pics and the stage performance was memorable. Another take away from Shep's book is, "TERMINATE THE COMPETITION AND GET CUSTOMERS TO SAY: I'LL BE BACK." When I went home that night, and for years afterwards I spent my money on Van Halen CDs, and still to this day I have a Van Halen channel on *Pandora*.

What is amazing, is the takeaway from each of my buddies standpoint. You have read how many times they each have seen Van Halen in concert. Van Halen gave them such a triumphant experience, that the guys and I were forever customers, and we were evangelists for Van Halen. We were the disciples spreading the word all around our school, teams, and our community, thus creating more raving fans. I know it was not only us, from Cleveland, to Dayton, to Columbus to Youngstown, to Akron, to Athens, the whole state of Ohio in 1984, was aware of Van Halen—because like Shep said, get the customers to say, "I'LL BE BACK."

EPILOGUE

Every single book I have written has had a message right away, a grabbing point as to why I was writing this novel—unbeknownst to me, very steadily as I delved into each chapter this book began to take form into what you have just completed reading. The original theme to the book was a Van Halen concert, and us guys got to see them—but like any idea, what starts off as good, turns into great.

This book was thought up by a seventeen year-old young lady, on a road trip with her dad to the Rock & Roll Hall of Fame—for months I composed ideas of how the book would read, I created a super rough draft of each chapter—then I would write the book based on various interviews I would conduct, that quickly was thrown out the door the minute I walked into Chris Berger's house back on November 5, of 2022. I was instantly drawn back into our youth the minute I saw him, and he saw me—big hug in the door frame. We had not skipped a beat.

We sat there for at least two hours jibber jabbing about his dad, my dad, about us both losing our moms, and the well-being of our fathers. The kinship was thoroughly present.

After leaving Chris house, where I had voice recorded our conversation, I quickly realized that this book needed to be written by six individuals, with a tour guide (Me) driving the Ford E-Series Van for this book to have any street credit. So, I sat down the next day and divided each section up based on the topics of which this book's chapters are laid out. I sat down and compiled the information, which was fresh in my mind down on paper, thus creating and changing the flow of this book. Each chapter is important in creating this piece, take one out and well this book never would have been generated.

As I am writing this part of the book, I have yet to play any interview that took place amongst all the folks in here, because I wanted to write my version of the story, what I remembered, what is still vivid and what is still clear to that year back in 1984—I didn't want me to "jump" on anyone else's journey, I wanted to share their memories, as clear as they could recollect. In so doing, I have only completed half of this book in my version, the other half goes out to all the guys.

I have never created a book this way, nor have written any chapter this way before, so this is a first. But in doing so, I have tricked my brain into not only describing what we all remember but recalling the friendship we all have. Sure, after grade-school, Chris and Todd went to Anderson High School, and Mike and I went to McNicholas. Each one of us creating our own journeys just like Van Halen did in 1984, going all over the country. Leadership and friendship is what transpired through writing this book, we are all tethered together forever because of that night, more importantly we all had a small part to play in the maturing into young adults that day—and today as we all are parents, that day is locked up in our vault, our lock box forever—no one can destroy what we all shared that day, no one can explain that day as well as us.

Van Halen gave all of us more than what we bargained for, that exceeded our expectations and then some—my friends in this book, are still my friends, my allies, and folks I am honored and privileged to call friends. The minute I called Chris about the idea for this book, he was on it, and we met up at his house. The minute I called Jim Jr up; he was all over it—we met at the library by his parents' house. The minute I called Mr. Myres up, we scheduled the next week, he fit me in, and for an hour and half he welcomed me in (No hugs Jimmy). Mr. Berger, same exact presentation, a firm hand shank, a guy hug and we were interviewing. Todd said immediately I'll be over to your house. Mike, on the other hand was hard to get a hold of. His son was getting married in Florida, so that took center-stage. We did finally get around to it, and he was 100% onboard, after I explained over the breakfast bar at Frisch's Big Boy.

"Life moves pretty fast. If you don't stop and look around once in a while, you could miss it."—Ferris Bueller. That quote is so uplifting, so hilarious to hear it and read it, because it is true—If Mr. Myres would have said no, we never would have gone. If Mr. Berger was not on patrol, we would not have been allowed to go—each person played an integral part, and if they said they were too busy, not enough time to go, then Van Halen never would have been seen in person. MTV would have been the only way to have experienced the four, but the dads didn't—they were 100% invested in watching us blossom, watching us crack our shells, hard to believe we were only in the seventh grade, well Jim was a junior, but still, Mr. Myres allowing him and his buddies to go off on their own, and us in the tenth row, the tenth row—WOW!!!!!!

Leadership comes in all fashions, Eddie was a leader and an influencer, as well as David (Just ask my mom), Alex and Michael were as well—leadership is something we all have in us, if we use it wisely, we will have a positive effect on others, if we don't, well I'll let your imagination fly. But to a be a leader of any sort, you must live by example—Van Halen is that example, if you firmly believe in your gift, if you continually hone in on it, master it and never listen to the nay-sayers, then the sky, (As they say) is the limit.

Friendship, was a funny word to me, when I was a young dad learning to express my wisdom to my daughter, through softball, karate, violin, soccer, rugby, vacationing—my mom used to tell me, "To have a friend, you have to be a friend"—that is so true, and when Maggie was growing up, sleepovers were always welcomed, movie theaters with buddies were encouraged, and hanging out with her friends was important not only to her, but to me.

As this book went off for its first round of editing, I was eating lunch with the Pieples family. There on their back porch while eating a Frisch's Big Boy, Gregg Pieples asked me If I was working on any new books? I said, "Yes, with Chris Berger." Instantly Gregg pepped up and said, "Berger! Was his dad a cop?" "Yes, he was," I replied. "I'll tell you a funny story about Mr. Berger," Gregg said. You know it's going to be good when Gregg starts off with that. "It was 1984, and Tommy (Gregg's young brother and my buddy in all the sports photos) and I were at a Van Halen concert at Cincinnati Gardens. We had nosebleed seats when we noticed a few empty seats down on the floor. So, we proceeded to take them. Half a song later, the rightful owners of the seats had us removed, then Tommy and I snuck around to another set of seats that were vacated, and sure enough their owners had us removed. Only this time ushers and the police escorted us to the back door and had us kicked out. The door slammed. Then the door opens immediately, and we hear this booming voice, "Tommy Pieples? What did you do?" Gregg goes on to say, "Mr. Berger yelled at us to get back in there and go back to our original seats. Which we did, and we got to enjoy the concert all because Mr. Berger gave us a second chance." Too funny not to share, friends all wanted to be at that concert.

Memories are why this book was written, but friendship is why this book was published. Never forget your old friends, never forget their parents, never forget your old neighbors, and never, ever forget your first concert—who you were with, where it was, when it was, what you were feeling—because forty years will come to pass, and that moment to you, will be pulled up through your subconscious forever and ever. Continue to *JUMP*.

Memorabilia

Chris Berger's Eddie Van Halen guitar pic—the one from the 1984 concert at Cincinnati Gardens. Given to him by Eddie Van Halen.

Chris Berger's Eddie Van Halen guitar pic—the front logo of the pic, received by Chris the night of the concert in 1984, at Cincinnati Gardens.

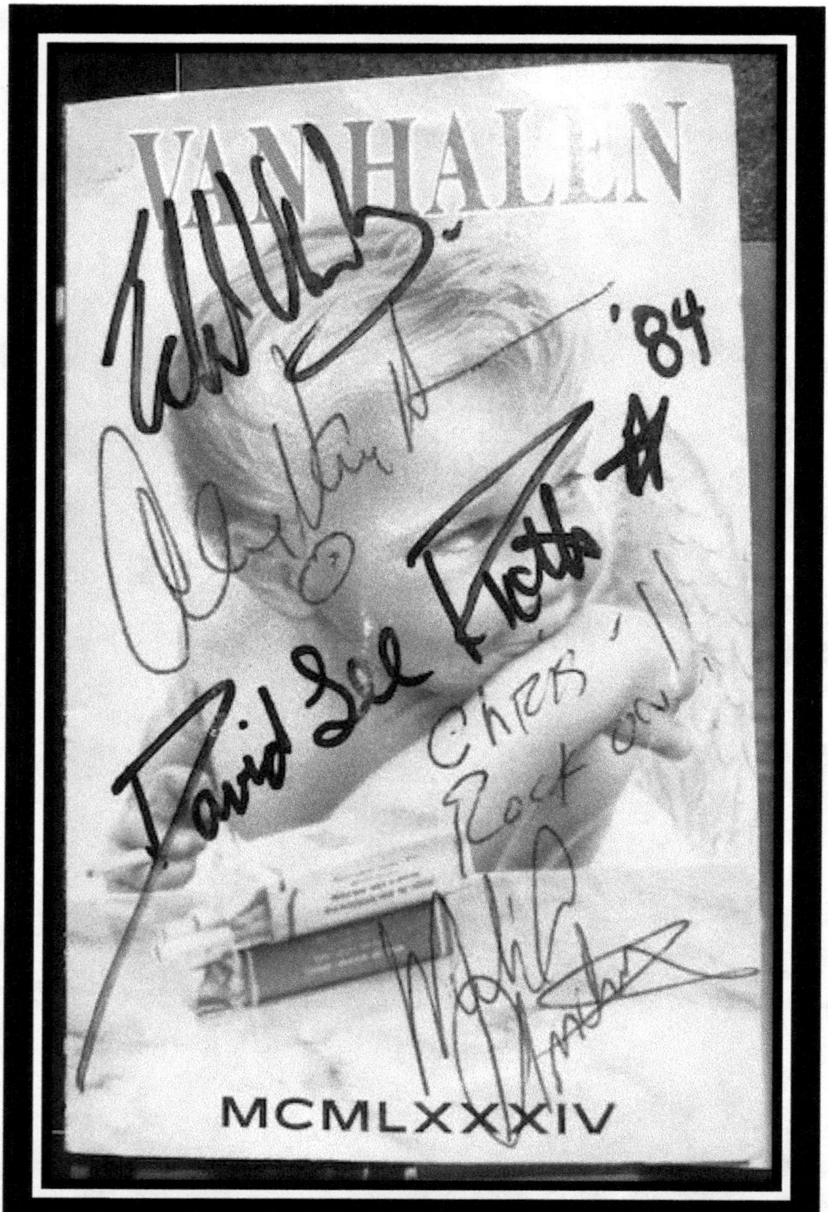

VANHALEN
David Lee Roth
'84
Chris
Rock on!!
MCMLXXXIV

When Chris Berger was told he was allowed to attend the concert, he took with him his *1984* cassette cover. When he met the band with his dad, he was all set to receive autographs. Sure enough, as Van Halen said to his dad, Chris was well taken care of, a gift to Chris as a thank you for the excellent customer service Skip gave the band. Notice that Michael Anthony signed this one, unlike the tour book. And, Chris got to shake their hands…..just amazing an experience for a thirteen-year-old. This one says, "Chris—Rock On!!"

This photo has never been seen before—Skip Berger took this picture. Eddie asked him if he would like to take some photos of him with the police detail group. As you can see Eddie looks to be getting arrested. The catch is, no handcuffs are on, he was just goofing around and having a blast backstage with the Cincinnati cops.

Eddie holding what appears to be a sniper rifle case, once again posing with the Cincinnati detail group backstage of Cincinnati Gardens. Skip Berger also took this picture. As Skip said in the book, "Eddie was a great guy." It fully captures Eddie's personality, understanding he had a job to do that night, he still took the time to play around with the very staff assembled to protect him, his wife, and the band.

Chris Berger has saved this *Creem*

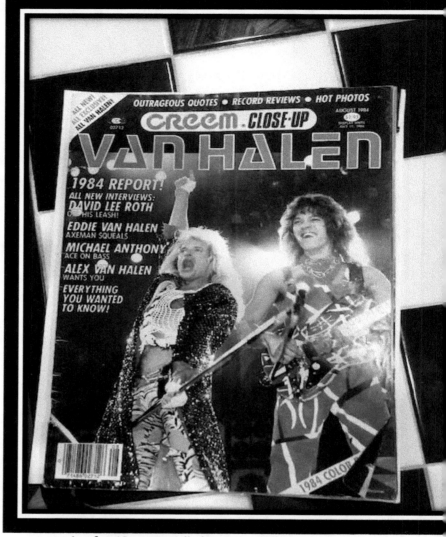

magazine for 40 years—all about Van Halen.

VAN HALEN MEMORIAL DAY '83

I asked Jimmy Myres if he had any Van Halen memorabilia—he said, "Give me a few days in the basement." Sure enough, Jimmy came through with this
post card from Van Halen—Jimmy has saved it for 41 years—1983.

One of multiple t-shirts Jimmy Myres has of Van Halen. It is completely worn out, as he proudly wore it forty-years ago. Notice that there are no sleeves, so Jimmy could show off his cannons to the ladies.

The back of the same t-shirt. Letting everyone behind you know
how you feel about Van Halen.

Another t-shirt of Jimmy's—notice the collar is completely worn out. But hey, this t-shirt is over forty-years old—Jimmy saved it all these years. Just awesome.

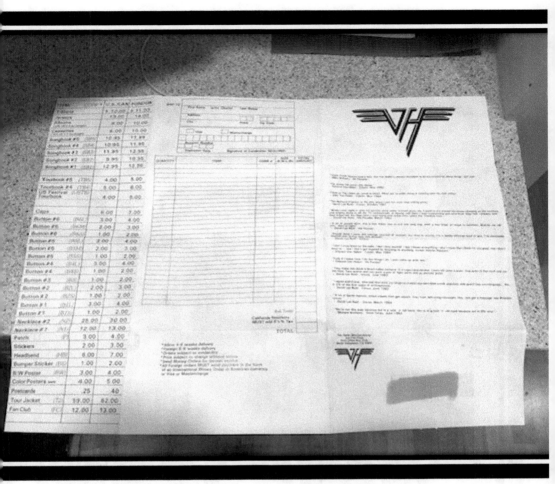

This just blows my mind—Jimmy Myres' Van Halen merchandising and fan club form, which was mailed to him. Crazy, in that Jimmy still has this in his possession forty-years later. One hell of a Van Halen fan.

The inside of Jimmy's merchandise form—in which you could order t-shirts, posters, caps, buttons, songbooks, albums, jerseys, tour jackets, head bands, stickers, patches, and of course the famous Van Halen logo 14K Gold Plated logo necklace. The quality of the form is as if it had been mailed out yesterday.

Van Halen Makes Cincinnati Gardens Jump

BY CLIFF RADEL
Enquirer Pop Music Critic

Well, dang. Van Halen isn't going soft on us after all.

The group has a little bit of Yes and a smidgen of the Kinks in its big hit, "Jump." But at Cincinnati Gardens Thursday night for the start of a soldout two-night stand, the four man band came out with guitars blaring the best in nosebleed rock and roll.

THE CAPACITY CROWD of 9,941 reveled in Van Halen's excesses of volume and high camp. Leading the way on both counts was lead singer, David Lee Roth, the clown prince of hard rock.

Throughout the show, Roth could not make up his mind who he was. At first, he bounced and wiggled around like an extra from "Flashdance."

Once he got that out of his system, he strutted around in his skin-tight pants with the fringe down the legs. There he was acting like a cross between Ted Nugent and Davy Crockett. King of the Wild Frontier indeed.

Roth's acrobatics and contortions were the comedic high points of this night of hoots.

Review

For the introduction to the old school song, "Hot For Teacher," he slid on his knees across the stage. Ouch!

Two songs later, as the bras and panties tossed by his adoring fans landed in a heap at his feet, Roth went into his demonic routine for "Runnin' With The Devil." This tune, dotted with Roth's patented milk-curdling screams, ended with the lead screamer striking a devilish pose at the stage's end while being bathed in torrents of bilious green lights.

WANT MORE? Here goes: After telling the crowd they were a bunch of "rowdy" so-and-sos, Roth then invited everyone in attendance to skip the rest of the show and "go across the street and get drunk." What a classy guy. He didn't say if he was buying, though.

Moments later, Roth stood at the edge of the stage doing the bump and grind. What a hit he would have been in "Flashdance." David Lee Roth, what a feeling.

Roth's fellow travelers, Alex Van Halen,

Edward Van Halen and Michael Anthony were more sedate than the singer. Alex Van Halen played his drums with a modicum of finesse. Brother Edward, the band's guitarist, known every pistonhead rock lick there is to know, and plays them every chance he gets.

Anthony, the group's bass guitarist, assaulted his instrument Thursday night. He threw it from a tower of speaker cabinets. Then he jumped on it. Then he kicked it. Then, while the poor thing was moaning in agony, he picked up another bass guitar and rolled all over the stage with his hands around its neck. Then he stood up and grinned. How cute when he's mad.

The night's opening act was Autograph. As opening acts go, this one belonged in the nickle and dime category, minus the dime. The quintet went on stage without a sound check. The drums sounded like a disemboweled '57 Chevy and the guitars were so out of tune they didn't make music, they made noise. All this could have been avoided if the band had either stayed home in their hot tubs in Los Angeles or warmed up. But then, hey, it's only rock and roll.

Photo of either Eddie, David, or Michael from that night, back in 1984. Photo taken by Chris Berger.

Chris' Van Halen pin—saved for over 40 years.

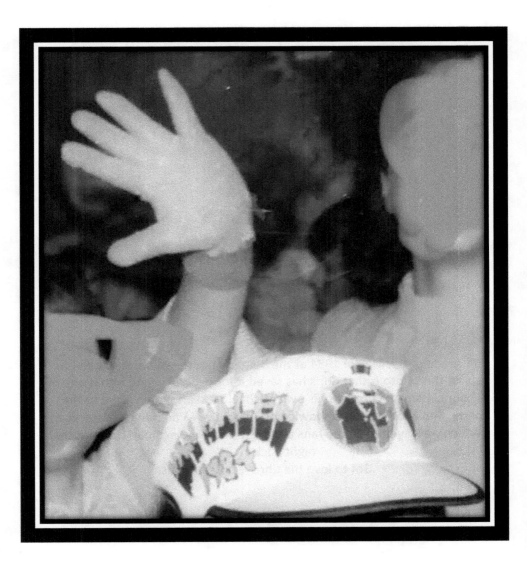

7th grade party, May of 1984 at the Berger's house—What is so hilarious about this photo is that Chris has saved it for over 40 years, is that one of our classmates brought his own Michael Jackson sequin glove to the party, and another one is showing off Chris' *1984* Van Halen painters cap. Which was given to all the fans upon entrance to Cincinnati Gardens that night back in '84.

Got to love the Chris' photo albums.

Jim Serger and his future wife, Gina. Dancing the night away in Skip Berger's basement back at the 1984 Chris Berger end of school year

BASH!!!!. Again, Chris' photo album comes through—showing all us guys had the moves back in the day.

INFORMATION

VAN HALEN

1. Van Halen http://www.van-halen.com/
2. Eddie Van Halen https://www.eddievanhalenstore.com/
3. Michael Anthony http://madanthonycafe.com/
4. Alex Van Halen
https://www.facebook.com/AlexVanHalenOfficial/
5. David Lee Roth https://davidleeroth.com/
6. Wolfgang Van Halen https://www.mammothwvh.com/
7. Sammy Hagar http://www.redrocker.com/

AUTOGRAPH

1.   http://www.autographband.net/

Other sites to check out VAN HALEN

1.   Van Halen News Desk https://www.vhnd.com/
2.   Van Halen Store https://www.vanhalenstore.com/
3.   Van Halen Shop https://vanhalenshop.com/
4.   The Mighty Van Halen https://www.themightyvanhalen.net/
5.   Wikipedia https://en.wikipedia.org/wiki/Van_Halen

Rock & Roll Hall of Fame

1.   https://www.rockhall.com/

ACKNOWLEDGMENTS

RECOMMENDED READING

Jim Serger graduated from the University of Cincinnati and was a Delta Tau Delta Fraternity member and served four years in the U.S. Navy. Jim lived in Japan for four years and served on board the USS Independence (CV-62). He has backpacked throughout Asia numerous times, climbed Mt. Fuji, and has completed two marathons (2017 and 2020). He worked at a little convenient store for six years in high school and college and in the packaged ice industry for 18 years after the Navy. Jim was an operations manager serving in the aviation industry for 7 years. In 2012, He rode a bicycle from Carmel, Indiana to Orlando, Florida for charity. Jim was a contributing writer to the *Current in Carmel* newspaper, from 2016-2021. Jim has written six books: *Go The Distance* (2011), *2000 Miles On Wisdom* (2014), *Next In Line Please* (2016), *The True Facts Trivia Game: For Fans of Fox News* (2021), A *Tale of Two College Graduates Who Landed The Interview: Amy and Jeff* (2022) and, *9:11 A Time to Always Remember* (2022). Jim currently is a Cincinnati Reds Usher. He is the proud father of a freshman in college and is married to the love of his life. Jim lives in Cincinnati, Ohio.

Printed in the USA
CPSIA information can be obtained
at www.ICGtesting.com
LVHW022327181123
764224LV00092B/4710